Financially Fabulous Divas

Handling Their Business and

Creating Wealth

All rights reserved. No part of this book shall be reproduced or transmitted in any form or by any means, electronic, mechanical, magnetic, photographic including photocopying, recording or by any information storage and retrieval system, without prior written permission of the publisher. No patent liability is assumed with respect to the use of the information contained herein. Although every precaution has been taken in the preparation of this book, the publisher and author assume no responsibility for errors or omissions. Neither is any liability assumed for damages resulting from the use of the information contained herein.

Copyright © 2019 by Lucille Tyler Baldwin
FinanciallyFabulousDivas@gmail.com
Financially Fabulous Divas, LLC

On average women shop
5.8 times a week!

Our Thoughts...
Rule our Actions

On average women own about 20 pairs of shoes!

I Am. I Can. I Will.

Dedication

This book is dedicated
to the many

Fabulous Women

who have touched my life in a positive way; women who helped mold me into the woman that I am today. They are the women with whom I share a bloodline. They are the women my mother calls friends; who have become my extended family.

They are my coworkers past and present. They are the nameless women who cross my path daily; women who make me smile and inspire me to do better. They are the special friends from my childhood: Connie, Lynn, and Marilyn; women with whom I share fond memories and lessons learned. They are the caring teachers from Grant School who saw the best in me.

They are the loving adults from my Miller Homes Community, "my village", that cared enough to chastise and nurture a young me. I will always hold a special place in my heart for Mrs. Margaret Mingo; one of the leaders of our neighborhood drill teams. Last, but not least, they are the women of Friendship Baptist Church who sprinkled me with love. In honor of my fabulous mother, Pauline Tyler, I raise my glass to toast the special divas that make me appreciate the solidarity among women. Salud.

***

Embrace Your *Uniqueness.*

Acknowledgement

Financially Fabulous Divas Handling Their Business and Creating Wealth has been dancing and sashaying in my head for well over a year, knocking against other books, vying for my attention, and trying desperately to get out.

It was through the unrelenting efforts of this fabulous diva that she was able to push her way to the forefront of my mind. It was inevitable that she would escape and make her way to print. She is my joy and passion!

I was moved by a Toni Morrison quote, "If there's a book that you want to read but it hasn't been written yet, then you must write it." *Financially Fabulous Divas Handling Their Business and Creating Wealth* is the book that was living within me. Each page represents, for me, all the fabulous women who have crossed my path and inspired me to move forward with the writing of this book. They gave me the courage to climb over my fears and insecurities to chase my dreams.

Once I started writing, the motivation to keep going always seemed to find me when I least expected - but needed it the most. It was in an encouraging word, a call from a loved one, or in a conversation with a passing stranger.

I owe an enormous debt of gratitude to all the women who have openly shared their financial struggles, stories, and triumphs with me. Your struggles are my struggles, your stories are my stories, and your triumphs are my triumphs. It is because of women like you that I am a better woman, and I thank you.

***

I am...She is...You are Worthy.

About the Author

I am a divorced mother of two who was sick and tired of living paycheck-to-paycheck. I was sick and tired of not having extra money set aside for emergencies or other unexpected expenses. I am also a woman who was tired of not being in a position to take advantage of financial opportunities when they came along.

I realized lack of preparation and especially financial information caused me to become dependent on credit cards and financial loans — also known as DEBT! I owed, I owed, and so off to work I would go, day after day, year after year, decade after decade to pay that debt I owed.

My awakening came when I realized that, like Dorothy of The *Wizard of Oz,* I unknowingly had the power all along to change my circumstances. I closed my eyes, clicked my heels together, and said to myself, *"I have the power to change my life, and I can do anything."*

I decided to take charge of my money and educate myself about personal financial management. On my journey to discovery, or my financial rebirth, I finally understood that it was my choices, and not my income or station in life, that would determine my wellbeing. I could continue to waste money on items that have no value, or I could learn to make money work for me.

In the end, Oz did not have the power to help Dorothy, and like Dorothy, I had to find my own way. If I wanted to have extra money for emergencies, it was up to me to start an emergency account. If I wanted to be in a position to take advantage of opportunities, I had to put myself in a position to answer when opportunity knocked.

***

SALE

Table of Contents

Introduction

Living, Loving & Growing With Our Eyes Wide Open

Dear Diary

My growth begins with accepting and respecting the girl that I was, the woman that I am, and the woman that is yet to be.

Right or wrong, I will take responsibility for the choices I make.

I will not be content to accept the minimum.

I would rather be hurt by the truth than to be protected with a lie.

I refuse to utter the words "I cannot" before I even try.

I will accept that the choices I make today will affect my tomorrow.

I went searching for happiness when I found myself.

Miss, Ms., or Mrs., I will always remain an independent woman.

I have learned that a broken heart will ALWAYS HEAL!

I will push through self-doubt, fears, and insecurities to become my best self.

I will not be defeated by procrastination.

Keeping a portion of what I earn is my only option.

I will overcome and learn from my mistakes.

If I only climb one rung at a time, I will eventually reach the top.

Who am I? I am what I say I am. I say I am fabulous!

I Am. I Can. I Will - With My Eyes Wide Open!

These shoes are made for saving!

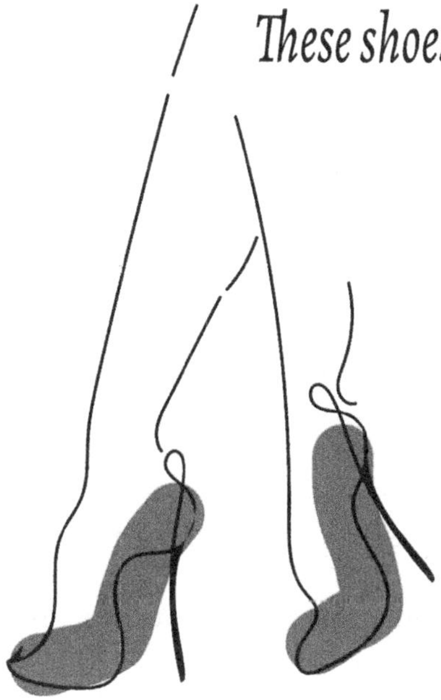

Living, Loving, & Growing With Our Eyes Wide Open

When I was just a girl, my mother would often say, "When people are voicing their opinions or giving you advice, you should listen to what they have to say. You should listen even if you do not agree with them because you just might learn something; or at least see the subject from a different point of view."

One of the worst things that we can do is to get to a point in life where we think we are beyond learning and growing, or believing that another person has nothing to offer or to teach us. Mahatma Gandhi said, *"It is unwise to be too sure of one's own wisdom...."*

Opening our minds and being willing to see things from different viewpoints is empowering. It is a wonderful feeling when we have an "aha moment" because of understanding someone else's point of view. It takes a special person to be willing to look through another's eyes and try to comprehend what they see without judging. The point is not to always agree but to at least acknowledge that life takes each of us down different paths.

We are all products of our childhoods. We drag around our experiences, clean or dirty, into the future. We all have a suitcase filled with our own personal chapters and verses. Some of us will pack stories of the perfect childhood, while others will pack horror stories because of dysfunctional families, abuse, or growing up in poverty.

Our experiences in life and the information that we received (or did not receive) hold the keys to our different points of view. Those views create the unique women that we become. Our experiences and uniqueness are what empowers us to bring different perspectives to the table.

Our responsibility as women is to be willing to grow with our eyes and minds wide open. We must be wise enough to realize that the more we learn the less we really know. This is a humbling realization.

I was talking with friends over lunch one afternoon and the conversation turned to the topic of our children and money. One woman shook her head in disappointment and mentioned that while her son and daughter-in-law both earn healthy incomes, they have no savings, no investments, and no money set aside for emergencies.

The problem is they closed their minds, believing that they were beyond learning or needing advice from anyone, including their parents. The last thing they wanted was someone telling them what to do with their money. By closing their minds, they slammed the door in the face of new ideas and possible growth.

We often complain or joke that men are too proud to stop and ask for directions. They would rather stay lost until, by chance, they reach their destination. We may be guilty of sharing the same pride when it comes to learning from other women.

Pretend for just a moment that hindsight is a superhero. Imagine that she has the power to give us the ability to foresee and understand the consequences and/or benefits of our everyday actions. Or, imagine if we could float outside of our neighbors' homes and peer through their windows, watching as they live their lives. After witnessing the outcome of some of their decisions, would you do anything differently? Would you hit the reset button and change any decisions that did not have a positive outcome?

What if a husband dies without life insurance, leaving his family to struggle financially? We learn, after the fact, that insurance would have protected his family from financial hardship. Would you learn from their mistake and make sure that you have life insurance for your family?

A stay at home mother of two is signing divorce papers without money to call her own. Would you learn anything from her situation? A father of four is laid off unexpectedly from his job and is without any savings or any assets. Would you learn that life happens and prepare for the unexpected?

If you believe that, like fashion, there is nothing new under the sun, then we can take comfort in the fact that any problem we may face, somewhere another woman has already gone through a similar situation.

If hindsight is an understanding of an occurrence after the fact, then learning from another woman's journey is our hindsight. Witnessing or hearing her story gives us the power to hit the reset button when it comes to our own lives. Who better to learn from than women who have gone before us? One of my favorite quotes is, "*Wise men learn by other men's mistakes, fools by their own.*"

The princess in us wants to believe that the bad things that happen to other women will never, and could never, happen to us. Why should we waste our time learning about money?

Unfortunately, most of us believe that talking about money is impolite and a topic that should remain private, or at least left up to men. We cannot afford to keep such an important subject buried in the closet or left to someone else. The problem with that is that at some point in our lives, 80 to 90 percent of us will find ourselves alone at a fork in the road, solely responsible for supporting ourselves financially! That is why it is important to understand that it could happen to anyone of us.

After my divorce, I found myself walking on that very road, carrying, what I like to refer to as my "Cinderella Mentality" neatly folded in my bag. My Cinderella way of thinking was that *love conquers all*, and that love was the key to living happily ever after.

I discovered that I was not alone on that road. I met a great number of women along the way and heard too many sad stories. I met young widows whose husbands died unexpectedly. Many of those women were left with little or no life insurance, forcing some to lose their homes. I met divorced mothers who found themselves suddenly plunged into poverty, often fighting for child support that may never come.

I met "daddy's little girls" and "mommy's princesses" searching for Prince Charming and women who found themselves in abusive relationships. I met women attracted to bad boys and I met young brides who thought their love and marriages would never end.

I met pregnant women whose husbands or lovers did not want the responsibility of a family and decided to move on. Some of the men moved on to other women leaving a mother to raise a child or children alone. I met displaced and replaced homemakers without any money of their own.

I met women who expected their pensions and/or Social Security checks to be enough to live on during retirement. I met women waiting for a Higher Power to make a way. Sadly, I even met the "other woman" who thought she was the better choice for her married lover, but also ended up alone.

The point is that I have met the eight out of ten women who never dreamed they would end up on that road - solely responsible for their own financial support. Regrettably, life does not always work out as we plan and many of us will find ourselves starting over.

If you think starting over is difficult, try enduring the emotional pain of a death, breakup or divorce. Add into that equation the burden of not having any money with children to feed. This truly is a difficult situation.

Imagine starting your life over in your golden years if you have not worked outside the home in a decade or more. Imagine if you do not have money or established credit in your name. I am sure we all know someone who has gone through a financial crisis and witnessed the resulting lifestyle changes. Remember: a *wise woman* is confident enough to learn from the mistakes of others.

Meeting Mr. Right and walking down the aisle is not a realistic game plan for financial security. Not only do we need to take charge of our finances, we also need to teach our girls to earn their own money, save, invest, and plan for a financially secure future.

We do a disservice to our daughters and set them up for failure by sending them out into the real world unprepared and believing in fairy tales. Enjoying "chick flicks" and fairy tales for entertainment purposes is one thing, but believing in them, and depending on their story line, is another.

A lack of money will limit our freedom, stifle our dreams, tie us to jobs we hate, and keep us in unhealthy relationships. Like it or not, it takes money to pay for the basic things in life such as a roof over our heads, food, clothes, transportation, medical care, etc.

Someone very close to me once told me, and not so nicely, "Money is not everything." I agree with her, but I also know based on experience, statistics, and listening to women tell their stories, *everything in life* is tied to the people we choose to love, health-related issues, children, education, shelter, and the almighty dollar.

The reality is that there are no crystal balls or palm readers that will allow us to peek into the future. How many of us have thought we found our Prince Charming, only to wake up next to a snoring Court Jester?

You and your partner share pillow talk. You laugh and gossip about your friends in the middle of the night. You snuggle and promise to love each other for life. To depend on love alone, however, will keep us trapped in a fairy tale.

In truth, the only person that we can count on 100 percent to take care of us financially is ourselves. There are women who will end up with the perfect life and never have the need to stress over money. There are women who will end up with one of the special and unique men who love and treasure them for life. There are also women who handle their financial business and could teach the rest of us a thing or two. However, there are far too many of us not prepared financially for real life.

All too often we tend to react after an incident rather than take a proactive approach. For example, we wait until our water heater needs repair then worry about the cost. We wait until we need to go to the dentist, and then worry about how we are going to pay. We wait until we need a new roof and then stress over the money. We wait until our relationship falls apart and then worry about making it on our own.

There are many reasons why women should know how to handle their finances. Still, the main reason is to maintain or gain financial independence. A realistic and common-sense approach to life is our best protection against an unknown future.

***

Chapter One

A Girl's Got to Have: A Little Black Dress & *Fabulous* Credit

"My life didn't please me, so I created my life."

-Coco Chanel

The Little Black Dress

Mademoiselle Coco Chanel, while she did not invent "The Little Black Dress," is credited with making it popular, affordable, and accessible to all women. An article in *Time Magazine* written by Sischy Ingrid, states, "Coco Chanel was shrewd, chic and on the cutting edge. The clothes she created changed the way women looked and how they looked at themselves."

Gabrielle Bonheur Chanel took her first breath in a workhouse/poorhouse in the Loire Valley where her mother worked in 1883. In 1895, when she was twelve years old, her mother Eugenie died leaving behind five children.

Soon after her mother's death their father, Albert, sent the children away. Her two brothers went to work as farm laborers. Chanel and her two sisters were sent to an orphanage in Correze, located in Central France. The convent of Aubazine where she was sent was founded to care for those in need: the poor, rejected, abandoned, and orphaned girls.

It was during her years at the convent of Aubazine that she was introduced to the art of sewing. When she left at the age of eighteen, she went to live in a boarding house that was set aside for Catholic girls.

It was at that time that Chanel began working for a local tailor. The name "Coco" may have come from her time spent as a stage performer. Two of the songs that she was known for are "Ko Ko Ri Ko, and "Qui qu'a vu Coco."

Chanel is known for: The Chanel Suit, The Chanel Jacket, Bell Bottoms, and Chanel No. 5 perfume. She is also credited with getting women out of restricted clothing and replacing them with comfortable and casual elegance, and of course, The Little Black Dress.

***

The Sexy and Sassy: First Lady Cash

"She walks in beauty like the night. Of cloudless climes and starry skies; And all that's best of dark and bright meet in her aspect and her eyes…."
-Lord Byron

The beauty of cash: there is nothing as comforting and calming as this reliable creature when you find yourself in a financial bind. Like a female ruler, the sexy and powerful **First Lady Cash** arrives to save the day.

It is an old adage that "we are known by the company we keep." All I can say is that this exceptional woman chooses her friends wisely. One of her closest and dearest friends is the elegant and clever **Lady Emergency**. Her associates know her best as **An Emergency Fund**.

It is the job and responsibility of **An Emergency Fund** to be there for us in case of a financial storm. She is smart enough to understand that building an emergency fund is extremely important in case of a job loss, illness, or any situation that interrupts our income or increases our expenses.

She also knows from experience that a loss of income will not put a halt to our financial responsibilities. Life as we know it, including those dreaded bills, will go on. By planning, we can ensure that our everyday living expenses, such as keeping utilities on, making the car payment, and putting food on the table will not be an added burden to an already stressful situation.

An Emergency Fund can only help us during a financial storm if, *and only if,* she is prepared. The fuel needed to prepare her is money and that responsibility lies with each of us. It may become necessary to sacrifice a few *wants* along the way to make certain that we can provide for her *needs*. Feeding her a portion of *all* that we **earn** or **receive** is the surest way to keep her healthy, happy, and strong.

It is lucky for us that the fabulous **First Lady Cash** has many amazing associates that we should welcome. She adores her childhood friends **An Asset** and **Wealth**. The three have remained devoted friends for centuries.

They hang out with successful independent women such as **Stocks and Bonds**, **Certificates of Deposit**, **Mutual Funds**, **Annuities** and other strong and proud women.

Her college roommate **401(k)** introduced her to the twins **Roth** and **Traditional IRA** at a Voter Registration Drive. They have become lifelong friends, often spending hours together discussing their financial futures.

What these fabulous women have in common is that they all have monetary value and the power to convert into **Cash** anytime extra money is needed.

Her Majesty — Queen Financial Knowledge, has dedicated her life to educating us. If we absorb the wisdom that she has to offer, we can defend ourselves against **Consumer Debt**. Our **Financial Freedom** depends on us eliminating him.

What can I say about those "**Bad Boys**"? The best time to prepare for a storm is while they are away and the sun is shining. **Bad Weather** and his friends can be childish at times. They think it is funny to create a rain shower or even a thunderstorm when we least expect it. They enjoy creating a violent disturbance of the atmosphere with strong winds, rain, thunder, lightning or snow. Those boys laugh wildly as they watch us scrambling to keep their mayhem from causing chaos in our lives.

The archenemies of **First Lady Cash** are the sly and sinister **Charge It**, **High Interest**, and especially, **Instant Gratification**. Which is the worst of the group. He wants everything *now* and refuses to wait and plan before making a purchase. He thinks waiting until you have the money to buy what you want is for chumps.

He would rather convince **Charge It** to buy what he wants now and then get his little brother **Monthly Payment** to be responsible for the debt. **Instant Gratification** does not care that it may take his little brother years or even decades to repay the debt.

It is the nature of **Compound Interest** to keep him making payments for years. **Compound Interest** and his friends are bullies and continue to increase the amount of money that he owes. For the moment, **Instant Gratification** is content with his new toys, that is, until a newer model comes along.

The women loathe **Consumer Debt**. He is the most powerful and controlling of them all and wants to keep us and **First Lady Cash** shackled to him for life. If he succeeds, we will become his financial slaves, spending years or even decades along with **Monthly Payment** trying to free **First Lady Cash.**

Because we owe him money that we have yet to earn, **Consumer Debt** is entitled to a portion of our *future* paychecks. He can be very dangerous, and because of our financial obligation to him, he can prevent us from becoming friends with women such as **An Asset** and **Wealth**.

***

Building Fabulous Credit: A Security Blanket

We need fabulous credit so we can have our own financial security blanket. Building and maintaining good credit gives you control over your blanket. You may want or need a heavier blanket or even an electric blanket to feel warm. When we give up control of our credit and finances, we must depend on others to keep us warm and secure.

Women tend to worry more about money and financial security than men. We have good reason to worry since we tend to outlive them, and normally have less money saved.

Another reason for concern, according to an article in the *New York Times* is that, "A record 40 percent of all households with children under the age of 18 includes mothers who are either the sole or primary source of income for the family." This is no longer Mike and Carol Brady's America. We must adjust our financial planning to reflect the changing world.

We may worry more about our security than men, but too many of us are still not comfortable, and do not handle our finances properly. The good news is that once we do take control of our money, we tend to do well and be more responsible than men.

Having fabulous credit in your own name can benefit the entire family; especially, if your spouse makes a poor financial decision and his credit takes a downward turn. It is also a good idea to have credit established in your own name in the event of an emergency.

Depending on someone else for your financial security is a lot of trust to place on another person's shoulders. Should that individual lose their source of revenue, it will be to your detriment.

As you begin building fabulous credit you may need to start small and prove to lenders that you can be trusted.

Begin by Creating a Positive Financial Paper Trail

- Open a savings and checking account in your own name and deposit money into the accounts on a regular basis. Saving even a small amount of money consistently will add up over time and show lenders that you have experience handling money.

- To help establish credit in your name, you can talk to the customer service representative at your bank about taking out a Credit Builder Loan. You deposit money into a savings account and take out a loan using that money as collateral. You cannot withdraw that money, however, until the loan is repaid. A secured credit card uses the same principle as a secured loan. Do not spend the money the bank lends you. Instead, deposit the money into your account and use it to repay the loan.

- Put a utility bill in your name and make sure that it is paid on time each month. If the day should ever come that you need to set up a home on your own, having a positive relationship with a utility company will benefit you. If you owe money to a utility company, you can forget about having lights turned on in your name.

- You will need to prove that you are responsible with money and credit. By getting a credit card in your name and making your payments on time, you can prove that you can handle the responsibility of credit. The purpose of the card is not to go shopping for bargains; it is to help you establish credit. Using it to pay a utility or cable bill that can be paid in full monthly will create the best payment method.

Start small and build your credit slowly. Never take on more than you can handle. Bad credit can take years to repair and repay. It also takes time to build fabulous credit. Do not get discouraged if it seems to be taking longer than you expect. It will be worth the time and effort.

The most important thing when it comes to establishing fabulous credit is paying your bills on time. Lenders have their own bills to pay and are not interested in excuses. By their standards, there are no good excuses. That includes the death of a spouse and the loss of a job. They expect you to be prepared for unexpected situations. So, build an emergency reserve and pay your *bills on time* if you want to build fabulous credit.

Be forewarned that credit is not to be taken lightly. If it is not handled responsibly, it can create a lifetime of debt and stress. The average American will spend their entire lives repaying debt while paying thousands of dollars in interest.

It is important to remember that the purpose of credit is not to give you the ability to buy items that you could not otherwise afford. The purpose of fabulous credit is to give you a link to financial assistance, when or if you need help making a major financial purchase such as a house, a vehicle or education costs. Having fabulous credit will also get you the best interest rates.

***

What Do Lenders Want?

Lenders not only want their money back but expect to earn a profit for lending you money. They do not know most of the people who come to them needing or wanting to borrow money. The only information they have about us is what they see before them in black and white.

They want to know what you are bringing to the table other than good looks, charm, or a sad story. They do not care how well-dressed you are, how nice a person you are, or how great a mother you may be. They do not care that you have children who depend on you. Lenders must determine from your "financial paper trail" and work history, how likely you are to repay the loan. This is not personal; it's just business.

Women laughingly tell me they are not good with money or that their partner is much better with numbers. I have learned over the years that our actions will take us in the direction of our beliefs. If we are of the conviction that we are not good with money - then we are throwing away our rights that women fought decades to win. Women in other countries are still fighting to gain many of the economic rights that we take for granted.

In honor of all the women who fought for our right to be independent, it is our duty to put our big girl boots on and stand up and handle our business. Building a strong financial foundation is not an option but a vital responsibility to ourselves and those who depend on us.

It was not that long ago that many women met with resistance when trying to establish credit. In some cases, creditors wanted a woman's husband or father to be responsible for the loan or line of credit. In other words—they wanted a man to be in charge.

In 1974 it took the *Equal Credit Opportunity Act (ECOA)* to force lenders to change the way they viewed women when making credit-granting decisions. Creditors will start with your credit report and credit score, not your husbands', boyfriends', partners', or even your parents'.

It is our responsibility to be prepared. The only thing separating us from the person sitting across from us is a little information - information that can be found in books and by asking questions. If you do not know - ask.

Even wrong questions will eventually lead to the right answers. Take one step at a time. Handling your money appropriately is not as hard as you think.

I always thought that chess was a game for great minds and too complicated for me to even attempt. I finally understood that the way to learn anything is by first being willing to try and then break it down to its simplest form. I learned the rules of the game and made up my mind to try playing chess.

I learned that the Queen is the most powerful piece; she can move horizontally, vertically, or diagonally by any number of spaces and attack from any of those directions. In chess you must protect your King at all costs even if it means sacrificing your other pieces, including your beloved Queen. The ultimate goal of chess is to put your opponent's King in an inescapable position to be captured. I may never become a Chess Master, but I no longer fear the game.

Financial Chess - The Money Game

The King may be willing to sacrifice his Queen in the game of chess, but that does not mean we should be willing to sacrifice our financial well-being for another person. Financial Chess is nothing more than preparing ourselves for real life. Learn the object and the rules of the game and then- **play to win**. The object of Financial Chess is to protect ourselves from financial devastation.

What lenders are looking for when they go over your application for a loan is the biggest question on the minds of most potential borrowers. What a lender learns from experience is that the people most likely to repay a loan are those who can prove they do not need to borrow money. These are people who own more than they are trying to borrow. They have land or other properties that could be sold to repay the loan.

If you own a house, car, or additional assets that the bank could sell to recoup their money you may be worthy of credit in the eyes of a lender. These items are known as **collateral**.

If you do not own anything that could be used as collateral, the lender checks your **work history**. They want to know if you have the ability to earn an income and are in the habit of repaying your debts. If the lender sees that, most will consider doing business with you.

If you do not own anything of financial value that could be sold and/or you do not earn enough money to qualify for a loan, you may need someone with good credit to be responsible for the loan. This may also be the case if you are new to the work force or have limited credit experience. This person is known as a **cosigner** and would be legally responsible for the loan if you do not, or cannot, repay it.

Finding someone to cosign and be legally responsible for your loan may be difficult. People willing to take on someone else's debt are rare. If you want to remain on good terms with family members and friends, then it may not be a wise move to ask those you care about to cosign a loan. Many friends and family members have parted ways over borrowed money.

Keep in mind that failure to repay loans can separate the best of friends and cause family dissension. Taking a family member to court over money will not make the greatest dinner conversation at the next family reunion. Depending on yourself to resolve your financial troubles is a great character builder.

***

The Value of Your Signature

To cosign or not is a very important decision that can affect your credit report. The person asking you to cosign is likely a desperate family member or friend. Someone you are dating may also put pressure on you to cosign for a car or money loan.

Since cosigning can affect your credit in a positive or negative way, it is not something to do without careful consideration. When people need a cosigner, they may use emotions such as tears or guilt to get your signature on a legal contract holding *you* responsible for their debt.

You should think of "cosigning" as "co-buying," because you will be responsible for repaying the loan if they cannot or do not repay it. Can you afford to pay for a car? Can you afford to pay for a television or washer and dryer? Can you afford to repay a loan? Do you want to become legally liable even if you can afford to pay? It can be difficult to get someone to make payments on time.

Depending on the state you live in, the creditor may seek payment from you first for repayment of the loan instead of the primary borrower. The creditor knows that you want to maintain your good credit.

Not only could you be responsible for repaying the loan but also for any late fees, collection costs, and attorney's fees. You could lose your property if you used it as collateral to secure the loan. The creditor may also try to sue you for repayment. The person who wants you to cosign most likely has bad credit and/or bad habits when it comes to paying on time. Let your friend or family member know that cosigning for a loan is very risky and can destroy your relationship.

***

To Lend or Not to Lend?

William Shakespeare's Polonius said it best when giving advice to his son, Laertes, in Hamlet: "Neither a borrower nor a lender be; for loan oft loses both itself and friend...."

To put it simply: the fastest way to lose both your money and a friend is to borrow or lend money. I have lent money in the past. It is not worth losing friends or the strain that it can put on relationships. There is an uneasiness in the air when someone owes you money. Before long, you start to resent everything that they buy while still owing you.

You think to yourself that they could have paid off, or at least paid on, their debt with the money they are spending. What if they do not mention or make an attempt to repay the loan? Should you mention the money? Should you remain quiet and pretend they do not owe you money? This can create a very awkward and uncomfortable situation.

It should go without saying that my answer to the question, to lend or not to lend, is NOT to lend, but thinking of saying no to a family member or friend in their hour of need can be stressful. It is difficult to say no when someone you care about comes to you for a loan. They always look sad and promise to repay you when they get their tax refund, next paycheck, rental deposit, lawsuit settlement, inheritance, Social Security check, loan from parents, money from their boyfriend, or even lottery winnings. You get my meaning!

The problem I found is that people who do not respect *their money* tend to have a hard time respecting *your money*. They also tend to believe that their financial responsibilities are more important than your financial responsibilities. When they get paid, get that tax refund, or settlement check, they tend to "need it" more than you.

Instead of repaying you, they may avoid you or give you excuse after excuse. Nothing, however, is worse than the borrower who gives you negative attitude or acts as though you are the enemy for wanting the loan repaid. If you ever want to witness the flip side of a friend or family member, lend or borrow money! Be forewarned, nonpayment of even small amounts of money can cause a rift. The ones you least expect can change from Dr. Jekyll to Ms. Hyde. If you do consider giving a loan, it should be an amount of money you can afford to give as a gift in case the loan is never repaid. You should not lend money you need for your own living expenses, or money that you depend on for emergencies. If you decide to lend money, then put the terms in writing.

***

Believe you can...
and you will.

Chapter Two

A Diva Needs the Perfect Shade of Lipstick & a Financial Umbrella

"Determination and perseverance move the world; thinking that others will do it for you is a sure way to fail."

-Marva Collins

Cause and Effect

We spend years preparing for adulthood: attending the right schools, meeting the right people, marrying the right person, giving birth to the perfect children and parking the right vehicle in the best neighborhood. The problem with that life map is that it is missing an important landmark.

Basic Financial Information

That one missing element — basic financial information — is **the cause** of many of our financial woes. A lack of such vital information affects our ability to make the best possible choices when it comes to money.

Because of that missing information, the average American is drowning in debt. Most of us are not prepared for the financial challenges of life. Some of **the effects** of a lack of financial knowledge are:

- Living paycheck-to-paycheck which is about 76 percent of Americans.
- Paying too much in interest and fees. The average American will pay an estimated $650,000.00 in interest over a lifetime.
- Student loan debt. Student loan debt in America has surpassed $1,000,000,000,000 (one trillion).
- Not being financially prepared for retirement.
- Bankruptcies. In America bankruptcies are at an all-time high.
- Not being prepared for emergencies. Approximately 27 percent of Americans have no savings at all!

A lack of financial knowledge is the *cause* and financial chaos is the *effect*. If we can change the cause, we can change the effect. Ralph Waldo Emerson wisely wrote, "Shallow men believe in luck. Strong men believe in cause and effect."

***

Let's Not Talk About Sex: Let's Talk About Money, Honey!

Let's put the conversations about Tom, Dick, and Harry on the back burner for just a moment. Instead, let us bring the topic of money to the table to find out which way our cash is flowing. If you have *nothing* to show for your money at the end of each month, then your money is flowing in the wrong direction. You need to figure out what you are doing wrong and make a change.

While on a financial treasure hunt and finding much of my money had been wasted, I was hit with a wake-up call. I realized my wasteful spending had been going on for years. Correction: my wasteful spending had been going on for decades!

In my case, purely by chance, while cleaning out my "miscellaneous drawer", I came across a stack of old checkbooks. As I was flipping through the check stubs, I was surprised to discover that I wrote four to five checks a week at the grocery store. I was spending hundreds of dollars a month buying small, unnecessary items. I would go into the grocery store to grab one item such as "a gallon of milk" and come out with $50 or more worth of items that I had not planned to buy.

Imagine my shock when I discovered that I was squandering hundreds of dollars a month! How could a divorced mother of two, earning a modest income, afford to waste hundreds of dollars a month?

The grocery store was not the only place that I was unknowingly wasting my money. I thought nothing of going to local retail stores to browse or to pick up one or two items. The problem was that I would again leave a store with merchandise that I did not plan to purchase. I was spending money that I should have set aside to pay bills, and/or to help fund my emergency account.

After going through months of old checkbooks, I discovered I was blowing over $300 a month! Once I understood that wasted money, it was a true revelation. Now, before going to the store, I write down the items that I want to buy or the amount that I am willing to spend. Sticking to a shopping list was difficult at first. With time it became easier and the money that I saved made it worth the effort.

To find your hidden wealth, you must go on your own treasure hunt. You may discover money that you are unknowingly wasting each month. The best way to discover where your money is going is to start keeping track of your spending. Tracking your money may seem tedious and time-consuming. However, if you want your situation to improve, then *a girl must do what a girl must do!* So, shake off all the excuses and just handle your business.

The good news is that you do not need a lot to get started on your treasure hunt. All you need is determination and a small notepad to jot down your daily spending. This first task will determine if you are Financially Fabulous Diva material. A Financially Fabulous Diva will take on the task even if she finds it to be a total bore.

If you hate the idea of writing down everything that you buy, you can simply keep up with your receipts. It is a good idea to track your spending for at least a month or two. A true diva knows that not keeping track of her money is unacceptable.

Anthony Robbins wrote, "In life, lots of people know what to do, but few people actually do what they know." It is like doing a "rolling stop" at a STOP sign. We all *know* the sign means to come to a COMPLETE STOP, but many of us choose to roll through it, disregarding the driving rules that we learned and know. Instead of blaming ourselves for choosing to disregard what we know, we blame the police officer for catching us and giving us a ticket.

We tend to do the same thing when it comes to our finances. We blame others for the financial chaos in our lives instead of blaming it on the choices that we make. Many of us know we need to prepare financially for life. The problem is that many of us make excuses and fail to plan. We tend to believe that financial planning is only for the wealthy or men.

I grew up believing the same thing. I assumed men were naturally better at math. I mistakenly thought that financial management was too complicated for me to understand.

I eventually learned that I could easily make my money grow by changing the way *I chose* to manage my finances. I realized that men are not naturally better at math. I watched in surprise as half of the young men in my math class dropped the course. I understood, after reading numerous books on personal finance, that creating wealth is all about common-sense decisions and has nothing at all to do with rocket science.

It turns out that I was not alone in my thinking. According to a report in *Time Magazine*, more than 40 percent of American women are now the family breadwinners. Yet, according to that article, we still "lag behind men in actions crucial to building wealth and security, such as investing and having a long-term financial plan."

***

A Major Emergency Fund

What if you had the power to look into a crystal ball and it revealed that your company was planning to lay you off within the next six months? What if you also learned that it would take you months to find another job? How would you choose to spend your remaining paychecks? Would you continue to create debt and purchase unnecessary items or would you start planning for those months when you would be without an income?

Three weeks after Christmas at a store meeting, the company that I worked for gave me the opportunity to peek into that crystal ball. That morning, the store manager informed us that eight of my coworkers were being terminated *effective immediately*. After years of loyal service, they were fired without warning.

They walked through the front door that morning with a full-time job and benefits and walked out two hours later with neither. The manager also informed us that they could return in two weeks and the company would be happy to rehire them as part-time employees, *without benefits*: no health, dental or vision insurance, no paid vacations, no 401(k), no sick or personal leave and no disability or life insurance.

Other managers were conducting similar meetings throughout the organization, affecting thousands of workers. It was a "win-win" situation for the company. They rehired returning workers with experience, while saving millions of dollars by eliminating their benefits.

Another instance happened when the employees of one of my favorite restaurants went to work one morning and found a sign with chains and locks hanging from the front door. The sign stated that the restaurant was "closed." Again, the job losses came without warning. Can you imagine the hurt and fear of going to work one day and finding the doors locked?

Consider the stress if you are living paycheck-to-paycheck. Through friends and coworkers, I realized that without a plan, I was clearly viewing a similar future. Full time American workers being replaced with part-time help has become the norm.

To avoid a similar fate, it was time for me to rethink my life and take a different path. We will rarely have the luxury of being warned about a loss of income. We can only learn from the past and the experience of others that the possibility is all too real and then prepare for it.

Building an Emergency Fund: One Dollar @ A Time!

Most financial advisors suggest having three to twelve months of living expenses in your emergency fund. With many companies closing and the growing number of jobs being lost, I like the idea of a twelve-month cushion. I know that twelve months may seem like a lot of money when you are trying to make ends meet, but *it is possible* with a plan.

The key to building your fund is to not focus on the big picture. It is hard to imagine saving a month's salary, let alone a year's. If you start out on a 5-mile walk, it would be impossible to cover 5 miles with one giant step. To reach your destination, you would take one step at a time. If you continue to put one foot in front of the other, you would eventually reach your 5-mile goal.

The same can be true for any task. It is often hard to accomplish a goal if you cannot visualize the undertaking in your mind. Instead of thinking in terms of saving a year's pay, or even a month's pay, start with an hour.

If you earn $10.00 an hour, then let the first step be to save $10.00, one hour's pay. Once you save your first $10.00, keep going until you save another $10.00. Now you have two hours pay saved. Keep putting one foot in front of the other until you have eight hours or a day's pay saved.

If you continue saving one hour's pay at a time, you will eventually have a week's pay saved. If you keep saving, you will have two week's pay saved. If you keep putting one foot in front of the other, you will eventually have a month's pay saved. If you keep moving and saving, the weeks will become a month; one month will grow to two; and two months will grow to three. The only way to cross the finish line is to keep moving toward your goal.

No more using the excuse that money is too tight. If you can only afford to pay yourself a quarter, then pay yourself a quarter. I do not care if you can only afford a penny; pay yourself a penny. The key to your success will be to keep paying yourself until your pennies or quarters become dollars. You will be shocked at how fast your money will grow once you take charge.

When you begin building your emergency fund, remember to set a goal that is within your reach. I never used to set goals for myself. I just allowed life to happen and then I reacted. When I set goals for myself now, I always take out a piece of paper and draw a ladder. I visualize myself standing at the foot of that ladder and I write down my goal at the top. Then on each rung, I write down the steps that I need to take to reach the top. Finally, I picture myself climbing that ladder one step at a time.

***

Learning to S-t-r-e-t-c-h Your Paycheck

A paycheck mystery—what is going on? We get paid and a few days later we have no idea what we did with our money. One of the best ways that I found to s-t-r-e-t-c-h my pocket money from paycheck-to paycheck is to give myself an allowance in cash. That cash must last me until my next payday.

One thing about spending cash is that you make a connection with your money. When you charge items, you cannot feel that money leaving your account. It almost feels like you are getting something free. With the swipe of a card, you take your items home. You swipe your card again and enjoy a nice meal. What the heck, you are feeling generous, so you pick up the tab and treat your friends. You had a great time and in your mind it did not cost you a penny.

Your coworker's little boy is having a birthday party, so you swipe your card again and pick up a specialized book with him as the main character. The next day you grab a sandwich, chips, and a drink during your lunch break. When you finally check your balance, you realize you overspent.

The great thing about spending cash is that you can see the money disappearing from your wallet. You may give a lot more thought to each purchase when you go from seeing $50.00 in your wallet to $20.00, especially if you still have a significant amount of time before your next paycheck. Bringing your lunch and snacks from home may seem a bit more appealing than spending your last few dollars on fast food.

Whether you are paid weekly or biweekly, you need to learn to budget your money. If you only have $50.00 to last you until you are paid, again it would be foolish to spend $45.00 on the first day. If you only have $20.00 to last you until you are paid again, you need to make every dollar count. The principle is the same whether you have $20.00 or $2,000 to last you until your next paycheck. Picking up dinner at a drive-through window should not be an option. What you earn is far less important than the choices you make with your money.

Wasting Our Potential Wealth

What do you own that has financial value? This was a question I had ask myself. It is an important question because most of us are not going wake up one morning and find money or rich men raining down and eag to take care of us financially.

A wise woman will keep up with the flow of her money for life. S understands that controlling the flow of her money will give her the pow to plug financial leaks. She understands that it is the small leaks like t $5.00 for a cup of coffee every day, the $20 spent going to lunch wi coworkers daily that can easily add up.

Wasting hundreds of dollars a month becomes thousands by the end each year and tens of thousands over time. It is money that could ha been used to help create wealth.

Here is a brief list of money sponges:

- Family
- Cigarettes, alcohol
- Impulse buying
- Designer Bags/Clothes/Shoes
- Too much partying
- Expensive vacations
- The latest gadgets, games, televisions, cell phones, – "must haves"
- Overbuying for children
- Cheap Jewelry
- Specialty Coffee
- Regularly Dining Out/Fast Food
- Unused Beauty products
- Gambling
- Consistently replacing cheap furniture
- Pets

Throw Away Clothing

"Throw Away Clothing" equals *Thrown Away Money.* There was a time when almost every household had a sewing basket full of needles and threads. If you lost a button on your shirt, or if you noticed that you had a hole in it, you would pull out your trusted basket and mend the shirt.

Today we live in a throwaway society. We drink a 16-oz. bottle of water and throw away the plastic. We drink a 12-oz. can of soda and toss the can into the trash or recycle bin. We purchase a new cell phone and once we become bored, we simply dispose of it without a second thought.

We spend all day searching for the perfect dress to wear to a party. We take a trip a month later and instead of packing that "perfect dress," we buy another.

Before long, both dresses are hanging in the back of the closet. They join the other forgotten and unwanted clothes destined for a landfill. All our unwanted clothes are eventually tossed on top of the 14.3 million tons of textile that we discard each year. The dyes and chemicals from the rainbow of colors in the fabrics that we abandon bleed into our soil, and the earth weeps.

Many major designers have brought their fashion to Main Street. They were given the choice to sell their clothes to a handful of wealthy women or to millions of middle class and working women. They reduced their prices and quality to sell to the masses.

Because the price of clothing has been dropping for years, we think nothing of buying, wearing, and throwing away our clothes. I never considered the harm that my buying and tossing was causing to the planet, other women, and, of course, my wallet. After watching the documentary, *The True Cost*, I now see the clothing hanging on the racks through new eyes.

The documentary reveals the price people around the world are paying so we can afford to buy, wear, and toss our clothes. So, before you go in search of another "perfect outfit" to buy and toss, check the back of your closet. You may just find the ideal but long forgotten outfit.

Vacation: The Forgotten Fees

Tips — Tips — and more people to tip!

Consider the cost of traveling to and from the hotel: Should you take a taxi, a shuttle or a private car? We paid $21.00 for three people to take a taxi to the airport, while two family members used a shuttle service and paid $60.00

Make time to research additional costs such as:

- Airline charges
- Baggage charges
- Wi-Fi charges
- Parking charges
- Food
- Check-in charges
- Occupancy charges
- Resort charges
- Late/early checkout charges
- Entertainment
- Port fees
- Pictures
- Tours

Brown Bagging: The Hidden Financial Benefit

The vending machine is the elephant in the room that fades into the background. Without noticing it, snack machines can easily gobble up your extra money. I would feed the machine at work a dollar for a sugary snack and a soda every morning and purchase another snack by late afternoon, giving up another dollar or two.

Everyone was doing this, so I thought nothing of it. My coworkers and I would sit around during our breaks laughing, talking, and enjoying this daily, very routine, bad habit. I misspent another $10 to $20 a day going out to lunch. What I was deducting from my wallet, I was adding to my waistline.

$12.00 a day for lunch and a snack (minimum)
x 5 days a week
$60.00 a week

$240.00 to $300.00 a month
or approximately
$3,120.00 a year

I wasted money little by little, one hour a day, five days a week, year after year. I squandered tens of thousands of dollars over the years during my lunch breaks that I will never get back. Unfortunately, there is no do-over for the money that I wasted. I made those choices based on my lack of financial knowledge and experiences.

As an alternative to eating lunch out every day and wasting money in the snack machine, I learned to do my wallet a favor. I started bringing my own brown bag/lunch from home along with healthier snacks. With the money that I learned to save by bringing my lunch from home combined with a little basic financial information, I was able to make different choices. Instead of spending money eating out and wasting money in the junk food machine, I learned that a little money could go a long way. The key is to keep a percentage of all that you earn for yourself.

If I saved just $10.00 a day instead of buying lunch

$10.00 a day
x 5 days a week
$50.00 a week

$200.00 a month
or approximately $2,400.00 a year

If I had paid myself and invested my lunch money in something as simple as savings bonds during my twenty plus years on the job, they would be worth over **$80,000**!

$50.00 a week x 52 weeks = $2,600.00
$2,600.00 a year x 2 (double my money with saving bonds) = $5,200.00
$5,200.00 x 17 years to mature (now takes 20 years to mature) = $88,400
or $5,200.00 a year x 20 years = **$104,000** (at maturity)

If I had only known, I would have been happy to bring my lunch from home.

***

Is Bottled Water the Superior H20?

Tap water versus bottled water: is bottled water really superior to tap water and thus worth the nearly $12 billion that we spend annually? Or have we been seduced by the bottling companies and their marketing agents?

We have been sold on the argument that bottled water is the pure and healthy alternative to tap water. The drink of the fit and beautiful people. However, the cost of bottled water is 560 to 2,000 times higher than the cost of tap water. Those selling the idea that tap water is unhealthy are the very corporations selling us bottled water and making billions of dollars.

I used to drink bottled water or "designer water" as some like to call it. I was sold on the idea that it was a healthier and better tasting alternative to the tap water. I enjoyed my designer water right up until the moment the news broke that the delicious water that I was paying for was nothing more than TAP WATER!

My designer water, from a major corporation was no better than the water that comes out of my own kitchen faucet. It seems that the company was not being truthful about where they were getting their water. After an investigation the company did admit to the deception. That information was released after pressure from *Corporate Accountability International,* a non-profit organization that helps protect consumers from corporate abuse.

The company is still selling their water and making billions. Only the phrase "Public Water Source" was added to their labels, when it fact it should read "Bottled Tap Water."

According to *Ban the Bottle*, an organization that promotes the environment by advocating a ban on one-time-use plastic water bottles says: "Making bottles to meet America's demand for bottled water uses more than 17 million barrels of oil annually, enough to fuel 1.3 million cars for a year and power 190,000 homes."

According to *Food & Water Watch*, "About 20 American universities have total bans on bottled water. The move to ban bottled water nationally continues to grow.

Soft Drinks: An Expensive, Unhealthy Thirst Quencher

50 POUNDS OF SUGAR!

The New York Health Department stated, "Drinking *one* soda a day equals 50 pounds of sugar a year." For our continued support of the industry, we get to drink liquid sugar when a glass of refreshing water would serve the purpose.

For decades, Americans have grown up drinking and loving soda, with 53 million Americans drinking at least one a day. If you are a proud soda drinker and you have absolutely no intention of giving up your beloved thirst quencher, then at least get the most drink for your money.

We do have options when it comes to buying soda, our most expensive option being the convenience store and vending machines. Instead, by buying a refillable mug, the cost of our drink would decrease substantially. Purchasing a bottle of soda from a convenience store on a regular basis should not be a first choice.

Another option is to buy soda from the local grocery store. We can gain the upper hand by checking store ads and buying it on sale, especially during the summer months or near holidays.

What do we get in return from the soda industry for our loyalty and the billions of dollars that we bestow upon them for a nutritionally nonbeneficial drink? We get to fill our bodies with 56 gallons of soda a year, and according to the *American Heart Association*, we also get to "increase our risk of heart disease, high blood pressure, and diabetes." Cheers!

***

Black Gold: The Coffee Craze Addiction

The coffee craze in America is alive and well. Americans are drinking 400 million cups of coffee daily — equivalent to an unimaginable 146 billion cups of coffee per year. A cup of Joe seems to be the way to start the day for many Americans as 65 percent of those 400 million cups are consumed during breakfast.

Coffee is the most consumed drink in the world, with over 50 percent of American adults 18 and over drinking their fair share. How much money are we spending on coffee each year? Let's use this as an example:

If a coffee drinker consumes three cups of coffee
a day at an average cost of $2.38:

$2.38 a cup x 3 = $7.14 a day

If you spend $7.14 a day x 365 days a year = $2,606.00

The average person will work for 40 years.

If we cut that in half and just say 20 years –

$2,606.00 x 20 years = **$52,120.00**

Our daily coffee consumption is another example of how we can make a small sacrifice and save a lot of money. Whether that means drinking one less cup of coffee a day or making your coffee at home, the choice is yours. Remember, we tend to throw away our potential wealth one dollar at a time.

***

Greeting Cards and Wrapping Paper

Greeting cards show that you care: they are that human connection; that hug in an envelope. There is no better feeling than opening your mailbox and finding a card among your bills. A paper card is more personal: you get to hold an item in your hand that a loved one or friend held and signed.

That warm fuzzy feeling may be the reason that 90 percent of people still prefer to receive their cards the old-fashioned way, by snail mail. According to the *Greeting Card Association*, "Americans purchase approximately 6.5 billion greeting cards each year. Annual retail sales of greeting cards are estimated between $7 and $8 billion."

Ladies, we purchase 80 percent of those greeting cards. We buy birthday cards, sympathy cards, wedding cards, thank-you cards, get-well cards, thinking-of-you cards, congratulation cards, Thanksgiving Day cards, Christmas cards, Valentine's Day cards, Mother's Day cards, Father's Day cards, and Halloween cards. We buy cards for every conceivable occasion and event.

If you are on a tight budget, consider reducing the amount that you spend on greeting cards. Budgeting 50 cents per card versus $10 per card can really add up over time. If you really want to make someone feel special, send a handwritten note.

Along with those greeting cards are often gifts that require wrapping. Knowing that wrapping paper will be discarded, we continue to spend about $2.6 billion a year on wrapping paper and gift bags.

According to *The Atlantic*, "As much as half of the 85 million tons of paper products Americans consume each year, apparently, goes toward packaging, wrapping, and decorating objects. Wrapping paper and shopping bags account for about 4 million tons of the trash we create annually in the US."

Every time you rip off a piece of wrapping paper from a gift, you are ripping up money. Every time you gather up wrapping paper from your living room floor and stuff that paper into the trashcan, you are stuffing money into that trashcan.

We would never wrap a gift with hundred-dollar bills and toss the money in the trash after opening the gift. Consider for a moment that we exchange *money* for wrapping paper and think nothing of throwing that wrapping paper into the trash. An alternative is to use newspapers, brown bags, or kids' artworks when wrapping gifts.

***

A New Year's Resolution: Getting Fit

A new year means putting our mistakes, forgotten goals, and missed opportunities behind us and starting anew; new habits, new goals, and of course, a sexy new body. If we are to take advertisers to heart, then a legally binding gym membership is the gateway to that sexy new body.

In a survey from *Bodybuilding.com*, "two-thirds of adults in the United States have made a New Year's resolution to become fit, but sixty-seven percent of those two-thirds gave it up before achieving their goal."

Like many Americans, I had the best of intentions when I committed to a one-year $55-a-month gym membership. I joined the sixty-seven percent of people with gym memberships who never use them, throwing away an average of $660 a year.

One fitness center added 100,000 new members nationwide in January at a rate of $35 a month. But it doesnot take long before the new members tire of the gym or health club and stop showing up.

So, who benefits from all the eager new members who pour into the gyms and health clubs every January in search of tighter abdominal muscles and flatter stomachs? The owners. They have learned from years of experience that new members are not likely to remain active for long.

Still, not all is lost. Millions of dollars will get a workout every month as they leap from our wallets into *the owner's* financial accounts.

Some gyms require contracts. Before you commit financially, make sure the time you spend at the gym will be worth the monthly membership fee. Try to commit to walking or working out at home before making a commitment to a gym. Weight loss takes more than an unused gym membership.

***

Dining Out: The Lost Art of Cooking

Just what is a girl to do when there are so many food options? There is fast food, frozen food, junk food, processed food, and fried food. There is food in cans and food in boxes. There is casual dining and fine dining. There are truck vendors and street vendors enticing us with food as we walk by.

We can have food delivered to our front doors and pay without cash. We can even order and eat food without getting out of our vehicles. Not only is food everywhere, but so are marketers and advertisers. We are consistently bombarded with images of beautiful happy people enjoying food and life. Advertisers would have us believe that the path to the good life is through our stomachs, where food and good times go together.

What they fail to mention is all that not-so-good food and the convenience of not cooking at home is making us sick, fat and in many cases broke. "Adult obesity rates have doubled since 1980, from 15 to 30 percent, while childhood obesity rates have more than tripled," according to an article in the *Trust for America's Health.*

We are learning that as much as we love eating out it is literally killing us when not done in moderation. The lost art of cooking is not only wreaking havoc on our health, it is also working its way to our purse strings. With thousands of dollars on the table, we should consider tightening our belts and investing in our families by reducing the number of times we eat out.

According to the *National Restaurant Association*, the typical adult will buy a meal or snack from a restaurant 5.8 times a week. Without thinking about it, the normal family in America eats out several times a week and gives little to no thought of the toll that it takes on their finances. On average, we can easily spend a couple thousand dollars a year or more dining out.

***

From Dining Out to Throwing Out

From the lost art of cooking to the woes of money wasted on food that we throw out or allow to spoil, it seems we cannot win with food. We either eat too much, pay too much or simply waste too much. According to an article in *Good Housekeeping*, "We throw away a third of the food we buy each week", i.e., a third of our money. On average we think nothing of tossing out between $500 to $2,500 worth of food a year!

Phil Lempert, CEO of the grocery information site, *Supermarket Guru* says, "We have a tendency to *overbuy and overcook*." Overcooking would not be such a bad thing if we ate the leftovers the next night or packed some of that food for lunch.

One step toward controlling waste is for us to commit to eating the food we have already prepared *before* we cook a new meal. We can save hundreds or even thousands of dollars a year by shopping with a plan in mind, along with that all-important shopping list. There is power when shopping with a list; it encourages us to get in and get out of the grocery store without adding unneeded items to the cart. Impulse buying is a budget and waste monster. Limiting the amount of impulse buying and time we spend in the grocery store can reduce the amount of food and money we squander.

Another step toward saving money is to compare prices ahead of time by shopping your local ads for bargains. My favorite bargains are BOGO, the buy-one, get-one free. Most stores will even allow you to purchase just one of the items at half price. Do not buy items that you do not need or use just because of a sale.

Freezing food is a great way to prevent it from ending up in the trash. The right storage bags and containers are inexpensive investments that can go a long way toward reducing food waste. Maintaining a neat fridge helps you to keep an eye on what you have and avoid the cost of duplicate purchases and spoilage.

Serving smaller portions may also help us to throw away less food. We often overestimate how much we will eat and end up scraping food into the garbage disposal. Our hard-earned money literally going down the drain!

Avoid the grocery store if you are hungry and/or thirsty. We tend to buy more junk food and other high calorie foods when our bellies are empty. Feed your stomach before hitting the stores. Otherwise, she will start making loud, weird sounds attracting unwanted attention. When she is hungry and begging to be fed, we tend to reach for those impulse items just to shut her up. We may pick up a chocolate bar or bag of chips, which is bad for our wallets and hips.

Your stomach is *not* your boss. Eat before going to the store and stick to your shopping list. Shopping with a full belly and a shopping list reduces unnecessary buying thereby saving you money and reducing waste.

***

Are you Smarter than your Phone?

When did the person on the other end of our phone become more important than the person sitting across from us at dinner?

Cell phones give us a freedom that we did not have in the past. Before the invention of the cell phone, we were only as mobile as the cord allowed. If we took the time to untwist the cord, we would gain another inch or two before we reached our limit.

How much is too much to pay each month for your cell phone? Only you know the answer to that question. Consider a few things. Are you funding your retirement account? Can you afford to set aside money for emergencies? Will you or your children struggle to pay for college? Do you have enough life insurance? Do you really need that smart phone?

Most of the people I meet think nothing of paying hundreds of dollars per month for their smart phones.

I often miss the "good old days" when people stepped into a telephone booth and closed the door. It was nice not being subjected to one-sided conversations, arguments, and only hearing the punch line of a joke.

Is the use of smart phones making us smarter, or is the use of smart phones making it acceptable to be impolite? Perhaps our smart phones should come with an etiquette card.

***

The Good Time Girl: Unplug and Save

Another month ends and once again it is time for me to fork over some of my hard-earned money to pay my electricity bill. When I turned off my lamp last night, I watched all the little red, green, and amber-colored lights, dancing in the night.

The television had a little red light that stayed on all night. The DVR also had a little red light that remained on. My laptop was glowing, with little bubbles bouncing back and forth. The light on the power strip for the television and DVR was a beautiful amber color. The light on my cable box was also the same yellowish-brown color. There was a green light emanating from the base of the cordless telephone.

My bedroom was lit like a 1970's night club. How can I call myself the boss of my domain if I allow my electricity to hang out all night like a good-time party girl? She was gadget-hopping from one appliance to another.

No more wasting energy and money; it is time I shut this party down. With one push of a button, I turned off the power strip: off went the red light on the television, off went the light on the DVR and the secondary cable box.

The next item to get the boot was my *ladylove*, my laptop, off with her until she was needed. My laptop was spoiled; she had grown accustomed to staying up all night.

Next, I put an end to other energy leaks such as the television playing when no one is in the room and turning off lights when I left the room or house.

The air conditioning and heating unit no longer heat or cool an unoccupied dwelling. Changing the AC filter every thirty days and replacing regular light bulbs with energy-efficient fluorescent bulbs was a major help.

I no longer waste energy and money washing one outfit. Reducing my energy consumption was as easy as flipping a switch. I reeled in my electric bill and all her little friends. By running my household like a business, I reduced my energy footprint.

The Cost of That Doggie in the Window

Celebrities have cute little dogs they tote around the world in designer bags. They are just so adorable wearing the latest tutu with matching polish. Forget about keeping up with The Joneses, dogs in America are trying to keep up with The Joneses' dog. For the love of Fifi and Fido, Americans are spending nearly $60,000,000,000 (sixty billion) a year on their pets.

If you are a first-time pet owner get ready for the cash to start flowing out when you bring your new doggie home. You will need to take it to the vet for a series of health checkups and vaccinations. These visits can become very costly. You do not, of course, want your dog to get heartworms, fleas, ticks, or other parasites. To avoid such pests they will need preventive medications.

Because dogs can develop human diseases, many vets suggest you do not feed your dog table scraps. So, add the high cost of quality dog food and healthy treats to your shopping list. How ironic that many of the foods that we eat and serve to our own families are not fit for a dog's consumption.

You know that you will need a leash and a collar. Where is your new dog going to sleep? Will your new dog sleep on a cold floor or a pet bed? There are other considerations. What are you going to do with Fifi when you want to go out of town for a weekend getaway?

Life happens! Dogs are hit by cars, get sick, and have medical emergencies just like humans. Our pets are like members of the family. If they hurt, we hurt. We are willing to pay almost any price to make them better.

Before you buy or accept that doggie in the window, be sure you are financially and mentally prepared. Most dogs do not come trained and that cute new puppy will need to be housebroken.

As we fight for health insurance in this country, it is readily available for that doggie in the window. You can purchase a dog insurance policy to help cover illnesses, injuries, and routine wellness care. That doggie in the window will require a lot more than a daily walk and a pat on the head.

Smoking: We've Got Our Own Cigarettes

"You've got your own cigarette now, baby — you've come a long, long way." In 1968, this catchy little slogan was written by Leo Burnett for the tobacco giant *Phillip Morris'* new Virginia Slims cigarettes.

Virginia Slims were the new bad girls on the block marketed to professional women who were ready to be a little rebellious. Virginia Slims represented independence, glamour, elegance, and any other adjective that would help seduce women into taking that first puff — and then another and another until they were addicted.

There was a time when women were not allowed to smoke in public as it was considered indecent. We may have come a long way when it comes to our right to smoke in public, but that right comes at a hefty price. Smoking is the leading cause of lung, throat, and mouth cancer and many other diseases. According to, the *American Lung Association*: "Smoking and tobacco use poses a serious risk of death and disease for women. Cigarette smoking kills approximately 200,000 women in the United States every year."

Every day, despite all the negative information surrounding cigarettes, about 4,000 young people under the age of eighteen try smoking, with about 1,000 of them becoming daily smokers. Teen girls often start smoking because they believe that it is glamorous, will suppress their appetite, and make them appear to be independent women.

If you smoke five cigarettes a day, then try to cut that number down to four a day-or better yet-quit. You can save the price of a pack of cigarettes a month. You can use that extra money to go toward your savings-*or health care!*

It may not seem like much, but keep in mind that our potential wealth will be determined by the small sacrifices and spending choices that we make daily.

***

Chapter Three

Stressing:
To Keep Up With The Joneses

Stressing: To Keep Up With The Joneses

What does "Keeping up with The Joneses" mean? It means to give away a small piece of ourselves to fit in with the so-called *"the right kind"* of people.

We may be giving too much power to a group of people who use designer clothes, expensive cars, luxury homes, and other material objects as their friendship-measuring tool. If driving a certain car or carrying a purse with a recognizable name is what makes you friendship material to some people, you may want to consider what value those people will bring to your life.

If we learn to be happy in our own skin, we can wear a two-dollar dress from a thrift store and be comfortable. Self-love gives us the power to walk into any room, with our head held high and our feet planted firmly on the ground, confident that our self-worth is not tied to our outfit. Our self-worth cannot be found on clothing racks or on car lots. Our self-worth and self-love, cannot be found in the approval of others but can only be found in the acceptance of the woman in the mirror looking back at us. She, alone, is our judge and our jury.

I used to be very shy until one day I found myself liking the woman looking back at me. I smiled and told her that I liked her and that moment changed my life. I discovered my best friend and I began my journey to becoming my best self. So, I say to you, screw keeping up with The Joneses. Our destiny goes beyond the judgment and acceptance of small-minded people.

If we were to peer into their homes, we may find that things are not always as they appear. The grass may look greener from the other side, but upon closer inspection you realize they used a spray concoction that only gives the false impression of a greener lawn.

Instead of trying to keep up with The Joneses, we should be minding our own business and handling the life issues within our own households. Like many of you, I could not understand why I was not getting ahead financially while others seemed to be thriving and living the American Dream.

I was running as fast as I could, yet I always seemed to be two or three steps behind my money. I spent decades chasing an unruly dollar with the heart of a wild stallion that refused to be tamed. I wondered, sadly, what I would have to show for a lifetime of work. It was then that my dollar whispered to me in a tender and loving voice:

"If I run wild, the fault is not mine. I have no power of my own.

I go where you tell me to go; I buy what you tell me to buy,

and I pay whom you tell me to pay.

You have taken chances and gambled me away.

You have forced me into machines to purchase junk food and sugary drinks.

You have left me crumpled and forgotten on the bottom of your purse.

You continue to separate me from my loved ones instead of allowing my family to grow.

You wander around stores exchanging me for items that have no monetary value.

In your search over the years for hidden gems and bargains, you walk by modern-day gold mines disguised as bookstores — not realizing that your strength lies within their walls.

Information can shine a light on your financial difficulties.

I remind you of a Chinese proverb:
'If you give a man a fish, you feed him for a day.
If you teach a man to fish, you feed him for a lifetime.'

My dearest one, if you learn to fish in the Sea of Knowledge, then I will remain by your side a faithful worker.

My children and my children's children will join me.

I have shared this information with others.

I have been called foolish and told that I should remain silent.
I have been called wise and have been thanked for my insight.

The doors to information are open to all those who choose to walk through.

Remember,

if I run wild, the fault is not mine.

I have no power of my own.

I go where you tell me to go; I buy what you tell me to buy,

and

I pay whom you tell me to pay."

-Money

"The future belongs to those who prepare for it today."

-Malcolm X

Payday:
The Reality of Your True Spending Power

Gross Income: Your total *income before taxes*, retirement plans/401k, and other similar deductions. Most lenders ask for your gross income when you apply for a loan, giving you the false perception that you have more money to spend than you actually do.

Net Income: Your take-home *pay after taxes* and deductions such as life insurance, health insurance, dental, vision, and retirement plans have been taken out of your income.

Disposable Income: Money used *for necessary living expenses* such as rent/mortgage, food, utilities, auto, plus debt that you are legally responsible for repaying. Disposable income can also be used for saving.

Discretionary Income: Discretionary income is the *money you have left over after you have paid your taxes, deductions, and living expenses*. Discretionary income is the amount of money that you can either save or spend on nonessentials such as entertainment, cosmetics, salon visits, etc.

Your true income is the money you have left over after you have taken care of business. We hear and see the gross amount of our pay and wrap our minds around that figure. You think to yourself "I make $50,000." That figure is not the true amount you have to spend on other nonessentials as mentioned above.

Choosing to block out the standard deductions and focusing only on the higher number, we mentally give our income too much power. Once you take a realistic look at your income, you get a clearer picture of just how far your money can really go.

So take your beautiful eyes off the Gross income amount, and take a realistic look at your Discretionary income.

***

The Disappearing Private Pensions

With the passing of each day, we are a day closer to retirement. Most people are not planning for retirement because they are under the false assumption that their Social Security benefits will be enough to support them. Although these benefits provide some income during retirement, Social Security benefits were never meant to be the only source.

Because of a lack of knowledge and naïve assumptions, Social Security has, unfortunately, become the main source of income for almost 50 percent of retirees. In reality, your monthly check will only replace about 40 percent of your earnings. Alone, it may not even provide a standard of living above the poverty line. Nevertheless, according to the *US Department of Health and Human Services*, 96 percent of all Americans will retire financially dependent on the government, family, or charity. Instead of spending money without thought, now is the time to start preparing for your future.

Social Security was meant to be a *boost* to your retirement savings and cannot replace a sound financial income. Most financial advisors state that you will need 75 percent or more annually of your current income to live comfortably in retirement; 90 percent or more if you are in a lower income bracket.

Not only is Social Security not meant as a main source of income, but our private pensions also may not be what we expected. The reality about private pensions, according to Cyril Brickfield, the former director of *American Association of Retired People (AARP),* is that "private pensions are in a state of chaos."

What does that mean for workers in the private sector? It means if you do not prepare you will have little to no income during retirement! It is vital to plan for your retirement and not wait until a year or two before the big event to think about retirement income.

***

Girls Just Want To Have Funds!

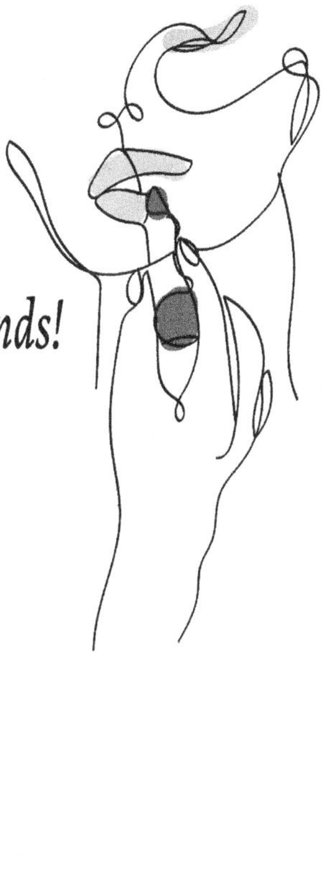

The Boys' Club Meeting

Unlocking the Secrets to Financial Empowerment

When we hear the word "secret," we tend to get excited, anticipating a bit of juicy gossip, such as the details of a lust or love affair exposed. Secret love affairs or other people's family skeletons should be of no concern to us — especially since we have our own skeletons rattling in a closet.

What should concern us, however, is that the *Encarta Dictionary* defines "secret" as "a piece of information that is known only to a few people and is intentionally withheld from general knowledge." This hush-hush information leading to success is the secret we should be sharing with friends and family.

Our elected officials should make basic financial information a requirement in all our schools. This would give each of us the opportunity to achieve financial freedom. No one can deny that understanding and applying basic financial techniques would empower us to make better decisions at every income level.

Is this lack of foresight on the part of our government intentional? Maybe. It is interesting to note that while the wealthy are getting richer, the poor are getting poorer and the middle class is rapidly eroding and losing its financial footing.

Perhaps men can lead us to the financial information we need. What secrets do the men know and share with each other that we do not know? Do we dare enter the "Boys' Club" and try to uncover the secrets to financial empowerment? I say we dare! Moments after entering the Boys' Club, we hit the jackpot: we found the minutes from their little black book. The very book that we all assumed contained the telephone numbers and star-ratings of women actually contains some of the information we need to achieve financial empowerment.

***

The Little Black Book

Page One: Gentlemen, under no circumstance is the information in our **Black Book** to be shared with women. It has come to our attention that men and women tend to spend, save, and invest their money differently.

In general, but not always, it seems that we develop our basic attitudes about money from our same-sex parent. Men learning their behavior from their fathers, and women from their mothers.

Women are usually taught to create a lifestyle for their families. They often focus on selecting the right furniture, the right linens, and the perfect china patterns all items to *beautify* and *enhance* the look and feel of her home.

Because of this learned behavior, many women tend to spend a great deal of money on items that have little to no financial value. They learn to create beautiful homes while neglecting their financial future.

Page Two: According to a report from the *National Council for Research on Women*, "Women constitute half of the US workforce and control more than 50 percent of the wealth in the US."

Women are also the heads of household or are the primary breadwinners in 4 out of 10 homes, and are therefore responsible for purchasing homes, autos, furniture, appliances, and groceries for the family.

Page Three: Talk about power! The financial power of women is like still waters that run deep. Not only do women play a major role in the US workforce and economy with their spending power, they also play a major role in shaping the character of our future generations.

William Ross Wallace's poem, *"The Hand that Rocks the Cradle Is the Hand that Rules the World,"* suggests that the person raising our children has the power to influence the character of those children and in most cases, that person is a woman.

Page Four: The power of women can be felt in all major areas ranging from the workforce, the economy, to the vote. A report by the *Center for American Women and Politics* states: "The number of female voters has exceeded the number of male voters in every presidential election since 1980."

Gentlemen, envision if you will, if women of all income and educational levels stopped doubting their influence and began to take control of their finances, voting power and influence over our children. They would be unstoppable! Women would rule the world. If more women understood their power, we would even be *forced* to pay them the same wages as us. Ha, ha! That, gentlemen, will never happen!

***

Women's Conference:
Changing the Financial Miseducation of Women

Good Afternoon, Ladies, and Welcome,

Today we come together in sisterhood. Now that we have exposed the little black book our goal is to motivate and empower all women to build a solid financial foundation through knowledge. Knowledge is the key to unlocking any door.

My hope is that by coming together today, we are moved to stand up and take action. My dream is that we find the courage and the strength of mind to climb up on the shoulders of the women who have blazed trails before us.

These women have opened doors, broken through glass ceilings, and dared to take the roads less traveled. We salute the pioneers who chose not to accept the limits placed on them, but instead had the foresight and courage to pursue their own dreams.

We can give honor to those women, past and present, by choosing to reach new heights to become our best selves. For many of us, choosing to become our best selves may mean breaking free from the safety of the crowd and doubters and making our way alone.

Albert Einstein said, *"The woman who follows the crowd will usually get no further than the crowd. The woman who walks alone is likely to find herself in places no one has ever been before."*

With every step that we take on the journey to financial enlightenment, we can rest assured that confidence will accompany us. Empowered with that confidence and financial information, we will no longer blindly accept everything we are told as truth.

We were told, "Girls are not good at math." We were told, "Women are not good with finances." We learned to distrust our own abilities because we accepted someone else's opinions as *fact!* Because of that *acceptance*, we unknowingly put shackles on our financial power — turning over our control and monetary responsibilities to others.

We learned to expect others to do for us what we are capable of doing for ourselves. We can easily rectify that by choosing to take back our power. With a little financial knowledge, we can begin to rethink our spending, saving, and investing choices.

The doors to the financial information that we need to create wealth are open. It is time to make our move. How we choose to go through those doors is up to us. Dr. Martin Luther King Jr. said,

"If you can't fly then run,

if you can't run then walk,

if you can't walk then crawl,

but whatever you do you have to keep moving forward."

Who among us is woman enough to rise above the opinions of others and walk alone if necessary? Who among us is woman enough to embrace unlimited possibilities by becoming our best selves? Who among us has the audacity not to walk, but to run through those open doors?

***

Mother, can I?

Yes, *you can!*

Why the Need to Change the Financial Miseducation of Women?

Because...

We shop when we are happy.
We shop when we are sad.
We shop when we are bored, and we shop when our hearts are broken.

The bad news is...

If that money was spent on items that have no financial value, then it is a lost financial opportunity.

The good news is...

We can replace bad habits with good ones.
The sun will come out again and the warmth will caress our skin and make us smile.
We will find someone or something to amuse us.
And yes, our broken hearts will heal.

Because...

Women on average tend to outlive men by five to seven years. The average age of widowhood is fifty-six years young. Many widows will find themselves in unfamiliar territory after the death of a spouse and clueless when it comes to handling financial matters.

Some widows will be left with less money than they expected and living in poverty will become their new reality. The average income for women over sixty-five is well below the poverty line.

Because...

On average women still earn less than men and often spend less time in the workforce because they are caring for children and/or elderly family. Less time spent in the workforce and for lower pay means less money available to fund Social Security and other retirement accounts.

Because...

Disagreements over money issues are the number one cause of divorce in America. After a divorce, a woman's household income level can drop by as much as 50 percent. The reality is that a divorced woman with custody of the children may find herself — with her children in tow — plunged into poverty.

Because...

Almost 40 percent of households headed by women live in poverty.

Because...

Unfortunately, some husbands, during a separation or divorce, may hide money, cancel credit cards, empty joint bank accounts, and even stop paying their share of household expenses.

Because...

According to an article in *Crisis Connections*, 85 percent of women who leave an abusive relationship return. "A lack of financial resources is the number one reason why women who have been abused return to the man who abused them."

Because...

Thanks to fairy tales, love songs, and love stories, many of us believe in soul mates and everlasting love. We expect our Prince Charming to love us, protect us and take care of us financially. In the name of love, some of us do not prepare financially for the possibility that the relationship may not work out.

Because...

The financial *miseducation* of women is causing too many of us to be unprepared for financial emergencies, widowhood, retirement, and other situations where money will solve a problem.

Before we make a purchase, we must start to ask ourselves: will this item have any financial value to me five years from now or will it be sold at a yard sell for a dollar?

Because...

The truth is that we are not natural born shoppers as our upbringing and advertisers would have us believe. To "shop until we drop" is not part of our makeup or in our DNA. It is learned behavior.

Because...

In real life, the road to "*happily ever after*" is not guaranteed. As women and mothers, it is important that we are prepared in the event our lives take a detour. We all want to think that the death of a spouse, a breakup, domestic abuse, or a loss of income will never happen to us.

Because...

Some of us, I am afraid, will be wrong.

***

You are...*Beautiful.*

This Land Is Our Land: The Power of Our Vote

Our Voices Matter. Our Votes Matter. Since 1980 Women voters have outnumbered male voters in every presidential election.

In 1848, Elizabeth Cady Stanton, Lucretia Mott, and Jane Hunt met in Waterloo, New York. Together the women planned a women's convention to be held in Seneca Falls, New York. The primary goal of the convention was to discuss the rights of women or, more accurately, the lack of rights for women.

*These women wrote the **Declaration of Sentiments and Resolutions,** which they modeled after the Declaration of Independence. **"We hold these truths to be self-evident: That all men and women are created equal and endowed by their creator with certain inalienable rights…"***

The Declaration of Sentiments and Resolutions detailed the "injuries and usurpations" that men had inflicted upon women. It also demanded, among other things, the **right to vote.**

Many of the activists and reformers were met with ***fierce*** resistance on their journey. Those against giving women the vote, and there were many, often heckled, jailed, and even physically abused supporters. They were not about to give women the right to vote without a fight.

It was with the approval of those against the women's suffrage movement that women were forced to submit to the laws of the land but had no voice in the creation of those laws. If a woman married, she lost all rights to own property. Everything she owned became the possessions of her husband including her wages.

The shame of it was that these men were fully against giving their very own mothers, sisters, wives, and daughters the right to vote. Many of the men did not consider women their equal and therefore were not qualified to participate in politics.

In 1895 the women of Massachusetts were asked by the state whether they wished the suffrage. Of the 575,000 voting women in the state, only

22,204 cared for it enough to deposit in a ballot box an affirmative answer to this question.

The biggest threat to the women's suffrage movement was the indifference of women themselves, according to an article published in the *Atlantic Monthly*, titled: Why Women Do Not Wish the Suffrage

"That is, in round numbers, less than four percent wished to vote; about ninety-six percent were opposed to woman suffrage or indifferent to it. This expresses fairly well the average sentiment throughout the country and can hardly be questioned.

There may be some western states in which the proportion of women who, for one reason or another, desire the suffrage is somewhat larger. On the other hand, there are Southern states in which it is even less. Certainly few men or women will doubt that, at the present time, an overwhelming majority of women are either reluctant to accept the ballot or indifferent to it."

It has been nearly a century since the passage of the 19th Amendment giving women the right to vote. Still many of us will lose our right to vote if supporters of voter photo ID laws have their way.

The changing face of America's voters has conservatives running scared to the point of extreme measures. They use scare tactics such as, alleged rampant voter fraud to change laws that will disproportionately affect the low-income, minorities, college students, the elderly, and yes, women voters. Voter fraud in America is almost nonexistent. Supporters of the law have been unable to prove that voter fraud is a problem in this country.

According to the *League of Women Voters*, "Roughly 90 percent of women change their legal name upon marriage or divorce. So, why the push for voter ID laws? The push has more to do with the changing face of the American voter.

People who normally do not vote showed up in record numbers in 2008 and 2012, a key factor in President Barack Obama's victories. Remarkably in 2008, 10 million more women than men voted which affected the outcome of the presidential election and helped fuel the voter ID laws.

"Just as grains of sand united can create a water's edge — one woman, one vote, one voice united with others can become a major political force."

-Lucille Tyler Baldwin

Did You Know?

- Susan B. Anthony and her brothers Daniel and Merritt were anti-slavery activists.

- In 1840, a World Anti-Slavery Convention was held in London, but because of their gender, women were not allowed to participate.

- Elizabeth Cady Stanton and Susan B. Anthony first met in 1851 in Seneca Falls, where both women were attending an anti-slavery meeting. Frederick Douglass also attended the meeting. He was a strong supporter of a woman's right to vote.

- The women began a lifelong friendship and spent decades fighting not only for women's rights, but also for the rights of all people.

- Anthony was very self-conscious about her looks, and even her speaking abilities. She had to overcome her insecurities to become a more effective fighter for equal rights.

- Stanton became the voice for Anthony's passion. She was able to write and speak what was in Anthony's heart.

- Many businesses were opposed to giving women the right to vote because they feared women would favor banning alcoholic beverages (Prohibition) and ending child labor.

- Child labor did not end because it was morally wrong – it ended because men wanted the jobs.

- Stanton also fought for birth control and parental custody rights for women.

- To ensure that his wife obeyed his authority and remained in her place a husband was *legally* permitted to physically abuse her.

- Women lost the right to own property when they married. Ownership of their property transferred to their husbands. In many cases, women had no voice in their own home.

- In 1860, largely due to the efforts of Anthony and Stanton, the *New York State Married Women's Property Bill* became law. The law allowed married women to own property, keep their own wages, and even have custody of their children.

- Anthony joined the teacher's union to fight for equal wages after she learned that male teachers were earning $10.00 a month while female teachers were only earning $2.50 a month. She also fought for equal educational opportunities for all people regardless of their race.

- The women's right movement lost steam during the Civil War (1861-1865).

- In 1868, Anthony began publishing a newspaper in Rochester, NY where she campaigned for equal rights for all American citizens, including former slaves. In her paper, she attacked lynching's, and racial prejudice.

- The 15th Amendment gave Black men the right to vote.

- Stanton and Anthony were against the 14th and 15th Amendment giving black men voting rights while women, both black and white, were still denied the right to vote.

- Anthony and several other women were arrested and found guilty of voting in the 1872 presidential election.

- Many of the Southern states were against the 19th Amendment granting women the right to vote.

- On September 30, 1889, Wyoming was the first state to give women full voting rights, even before the 19th Amendment.

- Women in Switzerland did not gain the right to vote until February 7, 1971.

- Stanton's father was a lawyer and had introduced her to law. She realized how the laws of the land favored men over women, especially married women. Stanton died in her home at the age of 86, in 1902.

- Anthony appeared before every Congress between 1869 and 1906 on behalf of women's suffrage. Unfortunately, she did not live to see the success of her endeavors. She died in her home at the age of 86, in 1906.

- The 19th Amendment passed in 1920 giving women the right to vote. It was not until 1980, however, that women turned out to vote in large numbers. That year Jimmy Carter lost the 1980 presidential election to Ronald Reagan.

The facts do not support the need for voter photo ID laws based on in-person voter fraud. The facts do reveal that because of the increase in voters among low-income, minority, college students, women, and the elderly, voter ID proponents are trying to prevent our votes from being counted and our voices from being heard.

***

Divided We Stand

The shame of a nation is to have poor in a land of
great wealth.
To have weak in a land of strength;
To have ignorant surrounded by information;
To have oppressed in a land of opportunity;
To have hungry in a land of plenty.

The shame of its people is to remain silent because...
the truth makes us uncomfortable.
they do not act like us.
their children do not look or sound like our children.
it is not our neighborhoods.
it is not our schools.
it is not our problem.
it is not our fight.

-Lucille Tyler Baldwin

Art speaks...

when words alone cannot.

Puppet Masters

What is *propaganda*? Propaganda is misleading or distorted information. Propaganda is designed to persuade us to think and act in a certain manner even if that technique is not in our best interest.

Edward L. Bernays, was the nephew of Sigmund Freud and was listed among *Life Magazine's 100 Most Influential Americans of the 20th Century.*

Bernays was a public relations mastermind. He believed that "We the public," ruled by our emotions and instinct could, and should, be led by those with money and power. He stated, "We are governed, our minds are molded, our tastes formed, our ideas suggested, largely by men we have never heard of".

Bernays understood that by tapping into our subconscious minds, our thoughts and spending habits could be manipulated. Corporations, politicians, and others could be *taught* to use marketing techniques, the media and public relations to mold our thinking, spending, and voting choices.

When a tobacco company wanted to increase their sales of cigarettes to women, they hired Bernays to do the job. Bernays convinced women that it was sexy and chic to smoke. Not only did he increase sales for the tobacco companies, he also convinced women that it was their idea and their right to inhale.

Bernays was well compensated for his efforts. The tobacco companies continue to make billions from the sales of cigarettes to women. Women also gained the right to get the not-so-sexy or chic diseases associated with smoking cigarettes.

The Puppet Masters are even turning us into armchair doctors. Between television programs, we are told to tell our doctors which drugs we should be taking. We often ignore the soft-spoken voice that describes the *many* possible side effects of those drugs which are often worse than the original ailments.

Have you ever gone into a store for one thing, just one thing, and come out with items that you did not plan to purchase? Have you ever disliked a political candidate because their opponent made derogatory *unfounded* comments?

Have you ever purchased anything because it is the latest fad and all your friends and neighbors, including "The Joneses," have one? Have you ever tried a new diet because a celebrity endorsed the plan?

How many of us have purchased an exercise bike or treadmill that has become a giant clothes hanger? We have all fallen for that fear of missing "a great buy" gimmick at least once in our lives. The sign reads for a "limited time only" or "last one in stock" our heart races - it is now or never! Before we know it, we are taking home another item that we do not need, usually creating another bill. It is the Puppet Master at his best.

Impulse buying has tapped into our subconscious. Our love of shopping and our fear of missing a great buy will keep us in debt. If we learn to understand what creates our love of shopping and impulse buying, we can learn to control our spending. Learning to cut the strings of the puppet masters will put us in control of our money. By learning to control our spending, we can work on getting off the paycheck-to paycheck treadmill.

The heads of well-known corporations know where their companies' money is going - down to the penny. These executives assemble regularly to come up with the best ways to keep expenses down even if that means paying less than fair wages, eliminating employee benefits, and outsourcing jobs. To them it is nothing personal, it is just good business. They are making decisions that will benefit *their* households, and *their* families. It will be in our best interest to do the same.

These companies can afford to invest billions of dollars bombarding us with advertisements, but they choose not to invest in their employees. They pay well-known celebrities millions of dollars to persuade us to buy their products, and millions more for airtime, print ads, and billboards to showcase their goods. Again, it is nothing personal - it is just "good business".

Propaganda Techniques: For the Love of Power and Profit

- Technique number one is convincing us to jump on the everyone-is doing-it **bandwagon**.

- We play the **follow-the-leader** game because our neighbors and friends are buying a product they saw on television. We read the same media-hyped books. We go to see the same "must see" movies.

  The Puppet Masters use **loaded words** or phrases. For instance, when the Bush administration used the expression *"weapons of mass destruction,"* it was intended to play on our fears. They used fear to scare us into sending our sons and daughters off to war. It turns out that there were no "weapons of mass destruction."

- The use of the phrase "***job creators***" has become common place to convince us that large corporations deserve huge tax breaks. They fail to mention, however, that many of the jobs they "*create*" do not pay a living wage or are created outside the USA. Do the so-called "job creators" really deserve huge tax breaks for creating low-wage, part-time jobs?

- **Testimonials** are another way to pull our strings. Advertisers suggest that because nine out of ten experts-in any given field-use a certain product or service we should trust them and use the same product or service.

- **Celebrities** make millions of dollars selling us beauty products — seducing us into believing that a cream can make our fifty-year-old skin look twenty years younger. Advertisers would have us believe if we drink the right soft drink it will fill our lives with laughter and good times.

- **Name-calling** and **ad-hominems** have become commonplace with politicians.

- Appealing to **The Grassroots** — This is where the suit and tie come off and politicians roll up their shirt sleeves to look like the hardworking man next door.

***

"Every great dream begins with a dreamer. Always remember, you have within you the strength, the patience and the passion to reach for the stars to change the world."

-*H*arriet Tubman

Chapter Four

Waiting for Prince Charming: The Financial Realities Beyond the Fairy Tales

"Don't settle for average. Bring your best to the moment. Then whether it fails or succeeds at least you know you gave all you had."

— Angela Bassett

Mirror Mirror

I do not meet the unrealistic standards of an American Beauty.
I have exceeded the ideal weight for my height. I have been called fat.
I have been called ugly. I have been called names
that I am too ashamed to repeat.

Some of the hurtful name-calling has come from
strangers, some from classmates, and
even some from family members.

My skin is pale. My skin is dark. I do not have the bluest eyes.
I am black. I am white. I am other: I am trapped between different cultures
and accepted by neither.
I am too light for one, and too dark for the other.

I do not own the latest designer bags. My shoes are worn.
I wear secondhand clothes.

My stomach is no longer flat. I have stretch marks. I have cellulite. I have
crow's feet. I have aged overnight.

My hair is straight. My hair is curly. My hair is coarse. My hair is
thinning. I am bald.

I am gay. I am straight. I am unsure.

I am uncomfortable around crowds. I do not fit in at school. I am different.

I am invisible - I walk unseen by the cool kids.

I am looking for love. I am unhappily married.

I am divorced. I am widowed.

I was replaced, my husband left me for another.

I am a stay-at-home mom. I am a working mother. I am a single mother.

My breasts are small. My breasts are large. I have breast cancer.

I have thin lips. I have big lips.

I have a gap between my teeth. My teeth are brown.
I have acne.

I have no family. My family is dysfunctional.
My father left us. My mother is a drug abuser.

I was adopted. I was abandoned. I was passed from house to house.

I was physically abused. I was verbally abused. I was molested.
I was unwanted.

I was called stupid. I was called a waste of a life.
I was told that I was useless.
I was bullied. I was neglected.

I am flawed and still

I Am Fabulous. I Am Irreplaceable. I Am Beautiful. I Am Woman.

I was born somebody

and

the world is better because I am in it.

***

The Power of Our Words

A Comment. A Conversation. An Opinion. Gossip.
The way we string words together and deliver those words have power.

Words…

CAN and DO hurt,
can attack, shame, or offend,
can make us give up,
can dare us to try things we should not,
can threaten and cause fear,
can make us hate,
can twist the truth into a lie,
can divide us.

Words…

Can turn a lie into the truth,
can make us thirst for knowledge,
can persuade us to change our thinking,
can hide secrets,
have the power to make us cry,
can make us believe good men are monsters,
can turn monsters into leaders.

Words…

Spoken or written, have the power to encourage, motivate, and lift,
can inspire and give hope,
can encourage us to dig deeper and give it one more try,
can unite us.

Like the seeds of a dandelion
words blown into the wind spread and take root.

Once Upon a Time in My Dreams...

I believed in fairy tales. I grew up watching amazing stories about Prince Charming and damsels in distress being rescued by romantic heroes. Through books and the magic of movies, I learned to believe that love conquers all. I was conditioned to always be on the lookout for my one true love — my very own Prince Charming.

With a child's faith I believed in everlasting love and soul mates. I expected my prince to ride up on his white horse, take me into his arms, and together we would ride off into the sunset, living happily ever after.

I thought that I met my prince; he was tall, dark, and handsome just like in the books. High school sweethearts, we would walk hand-in-hand under the stars, planning our future — two hearts becoming one — one soul, one love.

Several years later, we were married with two beautiful little girls living the "American Dream." According to the script, life would be perfect: our children would behave like the children from my favorite television shows. For a while, I thought life was grand, but I was just a naive young woman playing house.

After seven years, my not-so-storybook marriage ended in divorce, and I went from Mrs. to Ms. My fantasy never included a divorce or raising my children alone. The fairy tales that I read and the movies that I watched promised me a happy ending. My first love and I were not actors or make-believe characters in a book.

The problem with my childhood fantasy of marriage was that reality stepped in and surrounded me. My children did not come close to behaving like the children from the television shows. My prince abandoned his white horse and my rose-colored glasses were shattered as real-life set in.

The reality is that scripts can change, and "happily ever after" is not written in stone. I found myself alone with two young children, a part-time job, no savings, and no child support. I had become a statistic.

Looking back at the young girl that I once was, I realized that at twenty-one I was not prepared for marriage. I embraced marriage because of the power of great writers to tell magical love stories and the hypnotizing power of love songs. I was too young to understand that the movi directors and writers made a living creating perfect love stories. They too the average boy-next-door and turned him into a prince. My prince however, was just a man-child who was no more prepared for marriag than I was.

***

"In her first passion, a woman loves her lover, in all the others all she loves – is love."

-Lord Byron

The Big Day: With This Ring I Thee Wed

I wonder. Is our wedding day really the happiest day of our *entire* lives? Depending on how long we live, that could exceed well over 25,000 days. Realistically that is too much of an expectation to place on one day.

Perhaps it is just a great marketing ruse to justify spending thousands of dollars. I have often heard women say that they have been dreaming of their wedding day for years. The faces of their future husband may change, but their wedding plans remain the same.

Studies reveal that the number one reason many couples argue is money, which could eventually lead to divorce. So, which is more important to you: a wedding day that cost thousands or spending your life with the one you love?

Marriage is a new chapter in your life. You and your spouse are the authors with the power to write and star in your own love story. You can write stories that are filled with the difficulties that are associated with financial stress, or you can write a love story about a couple who works together to build a strong foundation.

We do not plan to start our new marital lives in over our heads with debt. It is easy to be carried away trying to live up to the expectations placed on your big day. Remember that wedding costs also can fall on your family and friends.

Spending hundreds of dollars for a dress that in all probability will only be worn once is a lot to ask of friends. Putting a financial burden on family and friends is especially sensitive if you already live with your future husband or have children together. Between credit card debt, student loans, and living expenses, they may be on a tight budget. What makes that day special is sharing it with the people you love.

Most engaged couples spend 50 percent more money on their wedding than they planned to, usually creating debt. In most cases, our weddings are driven by marketing gimmicks. We are told the best month to get married and how much the ring should cost.

We are also told which color gown is acceptable and we accept it as tradition. The fact is the color white was once seen as a color of mourning for French queens during the Victorian period. Sometimes we blindly follow the crowd without knowing why.

Queen Victoria is credited with brides walking down the aisle wearing white wedding gowns. Before white and lavish wedding gowns became "The Joneses" thing to do, brides simply wore any color they liked, with red being the "in" color of the period. Poor women tended to wear their best church dress when they married their true love.

Did you know that many of the wedding traditions we follow have a lot to do with fending off evil spirits? It was believed that wearing a veil would protect the bride from wicked spirits. The purpose of dressing the bridesmaids in matching outfits was to camouflage the bride and confuse the spirits.

So before spending thousands of dollars on a wedding, consider the real-life responsibilities that will be waiting for you after the *happiest* day of your life has ended.

***

Divorce:
What's Money Got to Do With It?

I love you — I love you not. I love you — I love not your debt. The number one cause of divorce in America as you know remains financial issues. It is easy to understand why because most of us have not been taught how to manage money. We bring our good, bad, and ugly financial habits to a relationship. If you want your relationship to be better than the average couple, then you need to come together for the good of the household, and in the name of love.

We know that the divorce rate in America hovers around 50 percent, with one out of two marriages ending in divorce. The divorce rate for second marriages jumps to 65 percent and that number increases to 73 percent by the third marriage!

Not merging credit card debt may keep down the stress of feeling responsible for your spouse's spending. It can also protect your individual credit score if your spouse has a habit of making late payments.

With all the new gadgets and technology, couples now have the power to track each other's *every* spending move. If you go to lunch with coworkers and use your card to pay the bill or stop to fill up your gas tank, your spending is being tracked.

Some may argue this point, but in my opinion, couples should consider keeping their consumer debts separate. The only debt you should have in common is a mortgage.

This will protect you from the irresponsible actions of your spouse. If your husband tends to buy a lot of toys on credit, let him be responsible for paying off that debt. If your wife/partner loves to shop and has a credit card for every department store in town, let her be responsible for those debts. The best way to come together is for both people to be debt-free.

Building or maintaining fabulous credit has **nothing** whatsoever to do with how much you love or respect your spouse. Building or maintaining fabulous credit has nothing to do with the financial IQ of your mate. It is just common sense — plain and simple. You never know when you may need fabulous credit or money. A financial emergency will not wait a few months until you have time to prepare.

I am a big believer in bringing reality and common sense to the table. The reality is that people die, lose their jobs, fall in and out of love, or simply discover that they want something or someone different in life.

A job loss or unexpected pregnancy can put a financial strain on a family. Suppose it is a difficult pregnancy and your doctor puts you on bed rest. What happens if you are a two-income household and your family depends on your paycheck?

Imagine finding yourself in an abusive relationship and you are financially dependent on your abuser. Once again, keeping your financial affairs in order has **nothing** to do with how much you love or respect your mate. It has everything to do with self-preservation: protecting the Queen — yourself.

My mother always felt more secure having her own money. She liked to be able to pull out her own money when she wanted. I can remember hearing her say often, *"I cannot spend what is in someone else's pocket."* We cannot take love to the bank or use love to pay our rent or mortgage.

Money is fickle and has a habit of following love, lust, or passion. Where love, lust, or passion goes — so goes money and financial security.

***

Divorce, Children and Poverty

The negative statistics of the financial effects divorce has on our children are overwhelming. We watch celebrities and athletes go through divorces and form a belief that women have it easy after a breakup, with their ex-husbands footing the bills.

The reality is that after a divorce, a number of women, with their children in hand, can expect their income level to drop by as much as 50 percent, plunging them into poverty. On the other side, the divorcing husband's income can increase by 25 percent with his quality of life improving.

Unfortunately, a divorcing woman may or may not receive child support. It is an unfortunate truth that only about 50 percent of all court-ordered child support is received, and only 25 percent of that is paid in full.

Because of an unexpected drop in income, women and children are often forced to move out of their homes. Adding to the devastation of a family breakup, children may also be required to change schools, leaving behind beloved friends and teachers.

Do not wait until you are faced with a devastating situation to learn how to balance a checkbook, pay bills or what it takes to run a household. As intelligent women, we cannot continue to allow love to blind us to the realities of life or convince us to bury common sense. We give our fantasies of love too much power. Depending on love, we unknowingly set ourselves up for failure by relying too heavily on our husbands or partners for financial support.

It is okay to fall in love and still have a separate checking account. It is okay to be in love and still build and maintain excellent credit. You can be in love, have an emergency account, purchase assets, and be in control of your life and finances. You can believe in "*happily ever after*" while maintaining your independence and handling your business.

***

Chapter Five

Through the Eyes of a Man

You are...*Amazing.*

A Prelude to Intimacy - or - Not!

Short-term intimacy and hookups have become chic. The phrase "*friends with benefits*" has become a badge of honor — it is nothing personal — just casual sex. If we choose to lower our personal standards, we devalue ourselves giving disrespect the opportunity to climb over the fence and cross our paths.

Hollywood and the media would have us believe that giving ourselves to someone after three to five dates is a reasonable period. The so-called "*Reality Shows*" tell our daughters that sex is normal within minutes of meeting a man as long as he has a killer smile and a six-pack.

The consequences that the movies and media exclude regarding the "three-to-five-dates-to sex" rule include unplanned pregnancies, heartbreak, diseases, and a damaged reputation.

If we follow the short-term to intimacy rules, then a candlelight dinner on day one, a walk on the beach on day two, and a few hours playing miniature golf on day three would represent enough time to become intimate with a semi-stranger. In real time, spending less than 24 total hours with someone would constitute enough time to slip out of our little black dresses and lose a heel under his bed.

Whether we want to admit it or not, *some* of us become attached to our partner after intimacy, even if we considered it a casual fling. Women release a large amount of a hormone called oxytocin into our brain during intimacy. Oxytocin is a bonding hormone sometimes referred to as a "*love hormone*" or the "*cuddle hormone.*"

Men, on the other hand, have a lower level of oxytocin in their brain, and may feel the need to flee the scene after an intimate encounter. Some men cannot put their pants on fast enough after a casual fling. We become another notch in their belt and a throw away date.

Once upon a time, "dating" meant taking your time and getting to know each other, having face-to-face conversations. If we are honest with ourselves, we will admit that most of us are normally on our best behavior during the initial dates. We may wear a little more makeup, an extra dab of perfume, and laugh just a little bit longer at his jokes - funny or not.

We may not reveal our true selves to each other until *well beyond* the three to five dates window. Finding out after you are enamored that he is married with children is not cool. Nor do you want to discover after a casual night that he left a friend behind — first name **Contagious**, last name **Disease**. A few dinners and a movie do not obligate you to tip your date with your body.

***

Intimacy:
Through the Eyes of a Man

I found interviewing men for this chapter of the book to be both no less than fascinating — and more than heartbreaking. It was disheartening listening to some of their locker-room views without feeling a little sad for us.

The men, a little apprehensive at first, were willing to break the "Man Code" and share their thoughts with a member of the opposite sex — as long as I was willing to listen without judging. The longer they spoke the wider the floodgates opened, and the more they were willing to share.

They spoke with such honesty and severity that I found myself wondering if they even like us. I must admit it was difficult listening to them speak about women in such a candid way without getting upset. They wore their lack of respect for women proudly on their sleeves.

They admitted freely their double standards are not fair and they do not care. They believe it is a man's world and women should just accept that as reality.

This is not the thinking of all men. To learn, we must be willing to listen even if we do not agree. Do not be offended. Living, loving, and growing with our eyes wide open empowers us to make better choices.

What did these men have to say about women?

- "Most women will do *anything* to have a man. They will even pursue married men."

- "Getting the girl is a challenge, like winning a football or basketball game. You win bragging rights and move on to the next game, or woman."

- "If I use the same line with every woman that I meet — I am confident that eventually even a ridicules pickup line will work."

- "Women go out to dance and meet Mr. Right. Most of my friends do not go to bars and clubs to dance. We go to bars and clubs to shop for easy or lonely women. Dancing is just a necessary mating ritual. It's like walking through the park – who the hell wants to "stroll" through the park unless it will eventually lead to sex."

- "When I approach a woman it is because I want to sleep with her. When I exchange numbers with her the goal is to get her in bed. She is thinking the same thing. We both know within minutes whether are not we will hook-up."

- "I am always honest with the women that I hook-up with. I let them know that I have a girlfriend — they can deal with it or not. If she doesn't the next chick will."

- "Too many women have low standards. They have no problem dating men without jobs, and men who have nothing to bring to the table. Some women with children will even move a man they just met into the home with her kids."

- "There are different types of women: you put them in a category according to the way they carry themselves, their conversation, and the way they dress."

- "Women say they want to be treated like a lady, but many think it is cute to get drunk in public and curse like men."

- "Some women say they don't want to be treated like a sex object, but they walk around wearing outfits that make them look like street hookers."

- "I get confused: women say they want a nice guy, but break up with the nice guy for a man who treats them like something on the bottom of his shoe. They claim that nice guys are too boring. They deserve the man they picked."

- "Some women don't know their worth — they are too grateful to have a man. They act too desperate."

- "I don't care if I have a hundred affairs, my wife or mistress better not have one — because I would dump her!"

- "A lot of women will stay in a bad relationship hoping or praying it will get better. They stay in bad relationships and label themselves 'victims.' Then you have the woman who does not learn from her mistakes. I don't want to call her stupid, but she will trade in one bum for another bum."

- "A man can hook up with different types of women: the one-night-stand female; the ones you will have to take out to dinner a few times first; the ones you call as a last resort; the friends with benefits. The sure thing is an ex-wife or ex- girlfriend that you string along for backup."

- "Some women care more about their new boyfriend than their children. They will leave their children with anyone with a pulse to run after a man or a party."

- "A lot of women are vulnerable. If you hold a woman's hand across a table, look into her eyes, and talk to her in a gentle voice for a couple of hours - she will fall in love. Trust me - it works every time!"

- "If a man cannot wait a year to be with a woman, then she should walk away from him. I will sleep with a woman on the first, third, or fourth date if she allows me. Hell, I will sleep with her in the first hour. I will also wait for a woman if I want a relationship."

- "I don't waste time trying a woman who looks confident, because I know I can walk around the corner and the next girl will accept a smile and a line."

- "Some women won't accept the truth. A man can stay out all night and not answer her calls. He can come home the next day with a 'good' excuse. She will make herself believe a lie!"

- "If a man loves you he will give you his name."

- "Let a man show you by his actions that he loves you. If a man slaps you or cheats on you, and then says, 'I love you' — you should run."

- "Some women are very judgmental. They judge men harshly by the car he drives, his shoes, or his job. They choose the guy with the expensive car. They don't consider that most of his money might be going toward a high monthly payment."

- "When a woman walks by in revealing clothes I will look! I may make a comment! I will smile and probably buy her a drink. What I am thinking is that she'll be an easy score. I am also thinking if she makes it easy for me, she is going to make it easy for the next man. I don't consider her girlfriend material."

- "Stop sleeping with us on the first night! Just because we ask does not mean you should say yes! I would love a million dollars. I can't take someone to a movie and dinner and expect them to give me a million dollars!"

- "If a woman sleeps with a man within a month or two — he will only hang around for a month or two!"

- "From my late teens and all through my twenties, when it came to girls it was just a numbers' game, another notch in my belt. I never met a woman I cared enough about to change."

- "Men put pressure on each other to score. The new woman in the office, the cute new freshmen arriving on campus, the new girl on the block, and women in general are all fair game."

- "My ex-wife was perfect. She was beautiful and took good care of our home and family. She even wore sexy lingerie to bed every night and I still cheated on her. My wife wearing sexy lingerie was like wrapping the same expensive watch in a different beautiful package every day. The package was beautiful — but it was still the same watch.

- "Love and sex are two different creatures. You can love one woman and still have sex with another woman."

- "It is okay for a man to have a wife at home and a mistress on the side as long as he is taking care of home. If I am also paying the bills for my mistress, she is not allowed to be involved with another man."

- "As long as I pay the bills I can come and go as I please. She can take it or leave it."
- "Women cannot do what men do when it comes to sex. No, it is not fair but that is just the way it is."

- "Some women take advantage of men, using them for money. The difference is that men can earn more money — a woman can never regain her virtue."

- "Hell no! She cannot stay the night! The last thing I want is to wake up next to her. I definitely do not want to feed her and have little "*Gremlins*" running around my house. Plus, if you feed them their emotions start to multiply and you will never get rid of them."

  "I normally think of an excuse to get her out *as soon as possible* otherwise she will be going through my s--- when I go to work. Or she will try to unlock my phone while I am sleeping. Sometimes I leave the house and have my roommate tell her she has to go."

- "Do not blame men! If she had any respect for herself, she would not go home with a man she just met."

- "Women pray for a good man. When they get a good man, they reshuffle the deck until they get an a--h---."

- "Some women look for good men in prisons and bars and wonder what went wrong."

- "Women make excuses to stay in dysfunctional relationships and then complain to their friends. Why would anyone choose to wake up every day miserable and hating their life?"

- "No, I would not leave my wife and family for a piece on the side. I just tell her that she is number two and she is satisfied."

- “Women pick the wrong guy and then try to mold him into the perfect man.”

- “Women tell me that I am too nice! What the hell does that mean?”

- “Women put up with disrespectful behavior that most men would never tolerate. If they don’t like the way they are treated, why do they stay in the relationship?”

- “Who am I to judge a woman for staying in a bad relationship? I think a woman who stays in a bad relationship has a good heart. She just needs a good person to take care of her heart.”

- “Women make the game too easy — there’s no challenge.”

- “Once you ‘date’ easy girls, it is harder to date nice women. The easy girls become addictive because they require very little work.”

- “I can get any woman that I want – even you. You would just take a little more work.”

- “The problem with easy chicks is that they often bring chaos to the table. Now you have trouble because you didn’t take time to get to know her. You find out to late that she likes to slice tires and key cars!”

- “The right woman takes work. It takes time to find out if you have anything in common. The woman you take home to meet your family will not accept the same treatment as a jump-off (a woman used for sex).”

***

You are...*Fabulous*

The Birds, the Bees, and the Boys

After hearing the not-so-nice things men had to say about women, I was curious to know what advice they would give to women.

QUESTION: What would you say to your daughter/sister about men?

I would tell my daughter/sister:

- **"TAKE TIME TO KNOW HIM** — get to know the man — get to know his character."

- "Plain and simple — some men will lie to get what they want, and what men want is women who will say yes. Do not be that woman."

- "Do not depend on a man to take care of you."

- "People often give us little glimpses of their dark side — do not dismiss those warning signs. Respect your female intuition."

- "If he is controlling, it does not mean that he loves you. It means that he considers you property that he owns — like his car or a pair of old shoes."

- "If he hits you once — HE WILL HIT YOU AGAIN! The only difference is that he will hit you harder the next time. His excuse will be that you pushed his buttons. You cannot fix him."

- "In the eyes of many men, a new female in the room is the same as a new gadget in the store."

- "Men always cry and beg to be forgiven or remember how much they love you *after* they get caught. Do not believe the tears. The new challenge in the game will be to get you to forgive him. If he is really sincere about being a changed man let him learn a lesson and become a better man for the next woman."

- "Men will only do better when women in general stop accepting bad behavior."

- If he tells you that he is not the marrying kind — BELIEVE HIM! If you do not believe his words, in time his actions will convince you."

- "It will take longer than one night or even a few months before some men reveal their true nature."

- "I would tell women that 'friends with benefits' — will BENEFIT HIM — more than it will benefit you. Do not make a fool's trade; 'friends with benefits' is like exchanging gold for paper."

- "Do not give up your dreams just because you meet a man — one has nothing to do with the other."

- "Do not be swayed by the car that a man drives or HIS money. You cannot drive HIS car or spend HIS money without HIS permission."

- "Men will not hesitate to tell you what they think you want to hear, even 'I love you.'"

- "Some married men will claim to be single. They will lie and cheat to steal your heart and use you without ever leaving their family. Their excuse will be that their wives do not understand them or that they are just taking a break."

- "What is his motivation? Is he looking for a relationship, a woman to take care of him, or a one-night stand?"

- "Do not put up with a dysfunctional relationship in the name of love."

- "Some men will take advantage of women when they are down. Do not exchange your self-respect for a helping hand."

- "Don't put yourself in a position where your survival is dependent on the generosity of someone else."

- "Do not allow your dreams to fade so that you can feed someone else's ego."

- "Don't believe that putting up with bad behavior from a man is what a woman is supposed to do."

- "Learn how to find the information you need to move forward."

- "Stop crying. Stop asking why. Stop blaming yourself. It does not matter WHY he cheated or hit you. What does matter is that you deserve better."

- "The more you love and respect yourself, the less s--- you will put up with from a man."

- "Do not create chaos and then blame others because your life is a mess."

- "It is not your job to make him a better man. You CANNOT create your dream man. Accept him as he is or leave him where you found him."

- "If you invest in a bra that was designed to push everything to the top — do not be offended if the product works and men are not making eye contact with you."

- "If you want to be treated with respect, then you must carry yourself with respect."

- "If a man calls you late at night, and that is unacceptable to you, let him know it is inappropriate and you will speak with him at a proper time."

- "The main thing I would tell women is to have a higher opinion of yourself. A man is not the prize. You are the prize. Stop chasing men and allow men to pursue you."

- "Most men will bend over and pick up a dollar they see on the ground. If you treat yourself like a lost dollar on the ground, then men/people will treat you with the same value as a dollar."

- "Do not be fooled; you will meet a lot of males in your life. Males look like men from the outside, but only time will prove if he is a man."

- "Stop trying to buy men with gifts and money."

- "There will never be a right time to be happy. You are not promised tomorrow. Get up and choose to be happy today."

- "Do not love blindly. Do not be a fool for love."

***

Girlfriend...

Get up.

Dry your tears.

***STOP** listening to sad love songs.*

You can breathe without him.

You can think.

You can eat.

You are somebody on your own.

You are not going to curl up and die.

You do not want to go blind.

The world has not turned upside down.

I understand that loving and not being loved in

return is painful, but love is plentiful.

Time will breeze through and eventually take away your heartbreak.

You can and will love again.

His loss was the greater — ***because he lost you!***

***

I Walked Away from *Love*

The night I walked away, our song was playing on the radio. It gave a sultry voice to our experiences; it gave dignity to my heartbreak and pain. It gave strength to every goodbye step.

I left because I was a woman-child caught between my childhood fantasies of love and the realities of a love gone wrong. I loved too deeply, too passionately, giving far too much of myself to a mortal man.

It was a romantic love. It was an idealistic love,
but it died a Shakespearian death.

It hurt to love with my heart exposed and unprotected from the pain of betrayal. He was my beloved, my childhood fantasy who gave me thorn covered roses that wounded when touched.

A thousand times I left him and a thousand times I took him back. With each return he brought with him a heart drenched with sorrow and a promise never to hurt me again.

I could not understand why I continued to love this stranger:
my prince, my foe.

Why did you take him back?

I took him back because it tormented my soul to remember the lover who was not in the bed beside me. I would miss the sound of his voice, the scent of his cologne, his smile, and his laugh. I would miss touching him and being touched by him.

When he returned, however, it hurt to watch him sleep each night wanting to believe that this time he would be different, knowing in my soul he would not be.

I took him back because I thought I could learn to break off pieces of my heart and give them to my lover sparingly. But to hold back what is owed to love is cruel - it imprisons the heart and depletes the soul.

I took him back because I thought I loved him.

I thought wrong.

I walked away because…

he did not value me.

I walked away because…

I knew I would never again be that naïve young woman who wallowed in the power of love.

I knew I would never again love with my heart wide open, unprotected from the pain of betrayal.

Sadly, I have learned to love differently. Sadly, I have learned to love cautiously.

***

*"Sometimes things fall apart
so that better things can fall together."*

-Marilyn Monroe

My mother told me that...

"A man will call or text a woman he respects before night falls.

If a man lacks respect for a woman,
he will call or text her in the dark of night with lust in his heart.

He will seek her company behind closed doors.

But,

when he walks out the door, he will long for her no more."

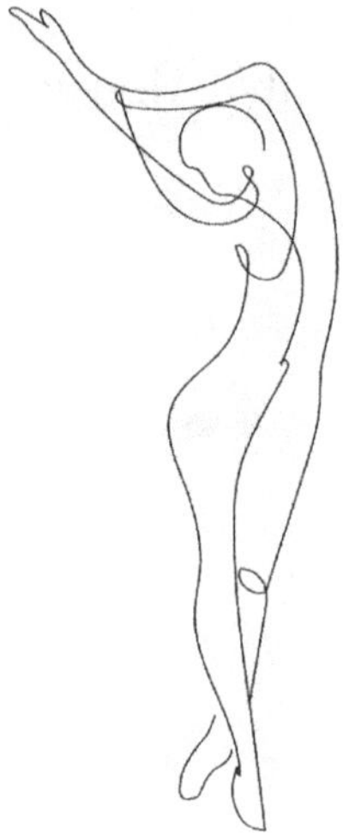

We sway to our own beat, and we are no one's...

Midnight Call.

From the Heart of a Mother

I know you think I worry too much and that parents just do not understand what it is like to be young. We worry because we understand all too well what it is like to be young. We understand what could happen if you make poor choices. We worry about you because we love you and we want you to be safe. We want you to live a long and happy life.

If you go out with friends, or if you are on a date — always have resources to get home safely. If they are serving alcohol at a party, never drink so much that you lose self-reign. You should always remain in control of your actions and aware of your surroundings. There is no such thing as a social drug or a social drug user. You do not have to take anything to have fun. You may not think it can happen to you, but drinking and driving, texting and driving, or driving while high can have a serious consequence on your life.

There is safety in numbers. Enact the girlfriend's pact. The girlfriend's pact is when you go out together, you stay together until you all return home safely. If you meet someone you like, you should make plans with him for another day. You should never break the girlfriend's pact to go off with him alone. Many young women have been hurt by someone they trusted.

I do worry about you moving too quickly with boys. Yes, you can become pregnant the first time. No, you do not have to be intimate with him to prove your love. Allow him to prove his love for you by waiting. Hitting and negative name-calling should never be a part of your relationship. Running behind a boy will not make you special — it will make you average.

Learning should not be confined within the walls of a school building. The opportunity to learn will cross your path daily. Taking special courses does not make you superior to others. A wise woman knows that wisdom wears different faces and comes in many colors. Bullies are insecure and lack true love. If you enjoy your own company, you will never be alone.

Always know that you are loved. The sun will rise, there will be full moons and beautiful sunsets to enjoy. There will be music and laughter. There will be books to read and awesome people to meet. There will be friendships to forge and dreams to pursue.

Be the woman who will make a positive difference in someone's life. Be the woman who shares a smile and a kind word. Be a thinker as well as a doer. Be the voice of reason and not the cause of dissent. Be the woman who puts her electronic gadgets away when she is in the company of family and friends. Be the woman who appreciates life. Be confident. Be independent. Be amazing. Be happy. Be you.

***

My Body, MY TEMPLE

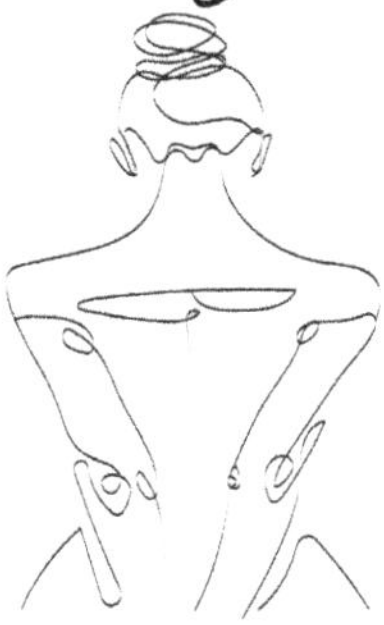

My mother may tell me and my father may warn me,
but ultimately the responsibility dwells within me
to honor, respect, and cherish my body, my temple.

It houses my heart and my soul.
It is the keeper of my mind and safeguards my private thoughts.

My Body, My Temple

It is not meant to be touched by angry hands.
How I choose to nourish and care for my body in my youth
will determine how it will repay me in my golden years.

My Body, My Temple

It is not meant to be given away freely to a smooth-talking Casanova
just because he utters the words — "I love you."
To be loose with my body may ruin my reputation and label me easy.

My Body, My Temple.

If I choose to honor, respect, and cherish my body,
my temple — why would I accept less from another?

***

Chapter Six

Money:

Raising Financially Savvy Children

"It is not what you do for your children,
but what you have taught them to do for themselves
that will make them successful human beings."

-Ann Landers

Unlocking Their Power

Our children have **E-N-O-R-M-O-U-S** spending power to the tune of **$200,000,000,000 annually!**

That money makes our children the perfect targets for corporations because they are young, impressionable, and have access to large amounts of money/credit.

The problem is that they lack the basic financial information to make responsible choices. This combination sets them up for financial failure. As a result, before they open the door and take their first step into adulthood, most of them have already created debt. The pressing question that we must ask ourselves is, have we prepared them for the real world?

Imagine the possibilities if we teach and encourage our young people to make some of that money work for them. The day will come when our children will move out of our homes and be required to make financial decisions for themselves. This includes buying or renting a place to live, buying a car, purchasing life and property insurance, starting and taking care of a family, and much more.

***

A Child's Plea

I will cry.

I will plead.

I will sulk.

I will suck my teeth and roll my eyes.

I may even throw a tantrum or two.

I know it may be easier to give into my tears and my tantrums in exchange for the bliss of peace and quiet.

I plead with you to stand firm against my tears and my bad behavior.

I will complain about schoolwork until it drains you, and you call upon a higher power to give you strength.

I will behave like that because I am young and I do not know better.

I do not understand the financial challenges that await me beyond my childhood as you do.

I do not understand that a good education can open doors.

I am only a child, and I must depend on you not to give into my actions.

I must depend on you because you hold the keys to my future.

My journey will be difficult if I leave home with poor financial skills such as spending beyond my means, never learning to save money, or lacking the ability to set financial goals.

My journey will be difficult if I never learn to handle credit cards responsibly.

In the real world, others will not love me as you love me, and they will not place life's necessities at my feet.

The advertising industry will spend billions of dollars per year on ads to entice me to buy their products and/or to use their services.

Depending on my television exposure, I can expect to watch at least 100 commercials a day and more than 40,000 a year!

Their goal is to raise me to become a loyal slave to their brands.

You have the power to delete billions of dollars' worth of commercials with the push of a button just by turning off the television.

The credit card companies will pursue me until I am shackled to them for life.

I look to you to provide me with the knowledge that I will need to shield me from their influences.

I am smarter than you think. I will understand if you explain to me the purpose of commercials and ads.

I will understand if you explain to me why I should start saving for my future.

I will understand if you explain to me the difference between a want and a need.

The path that I choose as an adult will depend on the lessons that I learned as a child.

I must depend on you to be my parent and not my friend.

I plead with you to prepare me for the day when I will leave home to stand on my own.

I plead with you to help me with my transition from child to adult.

I plead with you to be my voice when I cannot speak for myself.

I will hear what you say, but trust - I will emulate what you do.

Humph! I'm Grown!

I have reached the magical age of twenty-one, and now I'm Grown!
Oh, gosh - now what do I do?

People will expect me to behave as an adult and get a real job!

They will expect me to pay my own way.

I will need to eat to survive, which will require money!

They will start billing me for all those student loans, which will require money!

I will be expected to find a place to live, which will require money!

I will be expected to furnish my home, which will require money!

I will be expected to maintain my home, which will require money!

I will need my own transportation, which will require money!

I will be expected to maintain that transportation, which will require money!

I will want to go out and enjoy life with my friends, which will require money!

I may meet the love of my life. We will dress up and go out on dates, which will require money!

I may choose to marry my love, which will require money!

There may be children in our future, which will require more money!

There will be unexpected expenses in my life, which will require money!

I will want to retire from work someday, which will require money!

My time on Mother Earth will end, and even that will require money!

Someday We Will Spread Our Wings

In the blink of an eye the free ride ends. Parents will set us free to spread our wings and soar. The problem is that many of us have never really learned to fly.

Who knew that maturity and the ability to walk in the shoes of a responsible adult does not automatically go hand-in-hand with turning twenty-one? How do we become responsible adults if we spent the first chapter of our lives being catered to and spoiled?

How do we learn if our food was purchased, cooked, and placed on the table in front of us by loving hands? How do we learn if our clothes were bought for us, washed, folded and placed neatly in our drawers? How do we learn if all our needs and wants were handled by adoring parents? How will we succeed if we believe that the world revolves around us?

If we were raised in households where no one understood or appreciates the power of information, then life will be challenging for us. How will we survive if we never develop a thirst for knowledge? How will we succeed if we never develop positive work ethics? We will be set free to accept whatever life throws our way without question.

Some of us were raised in households that depended on the school system to prepare us for life. Some parents assumed natural instinct would kick in, and a good life would just start falling into place once we become of age. Some parents figured we would learn, as they did, by trial and error.

What will we do if no one instills in us the habits we need to thrive? If we leave home without a financial foundation and/or life skills, navigating our way through life will be a difficult journey.

Eagles know they must teach their eaglets to fly and hunt for food if they are to survive. A mother eagle will even go as far as allowing them to go hungry. She uses tough love to encourage them to hunt for food. She will also take the nest apart, little by little, thereby forcing her eaglets to become independent.

Just as soaring and hunting are not natural instincts for eagles, becoming a responsible adult, is not instinctive. We learn the skills we need by watching and emulating the adults around us. Once we reach the legal age of adulthood, people wrongly assume that we will know how to handle adult situations.

Many of us will learn the hard way about running a household and what is required to be a responsible adult. By the time we realize our mistakes, many of us will be thousands of dollars in debt and that debt may take years to correct.

It may be hard to believe at times, but parents are the most important role models in our lives. According to Randy Russac, a specialist in child psychology at the *University of North Florida*, children take on their parents' attitudes before the age of six.

The financial realities that await us if we are not prepared are not pretty. Inaction or doing for us what we should be learning to do for ourselves will only hinder us — even if it is done out of love. When we leave home, we will be responsible for doing our own laundry, cooking, and making sure bills are paid on time.

A car is probably the second most expensive item that will be purchased after a house. If we make a poor decision at a dealership, it can easily set us back years financially by locking us into high monthly payments.

Understanding the importance of building and maintaining good credit is of the utmost importance. Learning to take care of our credit and keeping a good credit score will be beneficial for a lifetime

***

Before They Were Rich

What do two very wealthy men think we should be teaching our children about money? Two of the most affluent men in the world have similar upbringings that we can easily emulate. Carlos Slim and Warren Buffett — the second and third richest men in the world, respectively, were both introduced to *saving money* and *investing* at a very young age.

Carlos Slim, was born in Mexico City. He had his own checking account by the time he was ten or twelve years old. Every week, Carlos's father gave him five pesos, which is worth less than 50 cents today. Carlos would spend less than he had and began to put the money he saved into a bank.

Warren Buffett grew up in Omaha, Nebraska, but shares a similar experience as Mr. Slim. Mr. Buffett's father opened his first savings account for him when he was six years old with $20. From that point on, Warren Buffett would save the money that he received from chores, and gifts. When he brought his account up to $120, he made his first investment. Mr. Buffett notes that his father "was a huge influence" on his life.

Mr. Buffett believes that "teaching kids sound financial habits at an early age gives all kids the opportunity to be successful adults."

Once children realize that money has the power to buy them the things they want, such as candy and toys, it is time for their financial lessons to begin.

A study from Cambridge University states that "adult money habits are set by the age of seven years old." This study tells us that the practices we hope to see in our adult children are the behaviors that we must instill in them while they are young. I was talking with a new mother about children and finances. She did not believe we had the power to instill in them healthy financial habits. She said, "We can only hope." We cannot rely on hope. We must rely on information and training!

Many of us give our children an allowance without teaching them how to set financial goals. When we give money without introducing the purpose of money, we lose an opportunity to implant healthy financial habits in our children.

The early decisions of Mr. Buffett and Mr. Slim are traits and behaviors that we can easily teach our children to follow. The amount they learn to save is not important. What is important is that we pass on healthy financial habits to our children.

***

Everyday Life: The Empowerment Game

What can we do to raise financially savvy children? We can make everyday situations a learning experience, from paying bills to turning off a light. Even a simple trip to the grocery store can be a learning experience. It is the perfect opportunity to talk to our children about the high cost of food.

It is also the perfect time to demonstrate the importance of shopping with, and sticking to, a list. One way to involve our children with the shopping is to ask for their assistance and to encourage them to help locate the items. A treasure hunt can be a fun way to keep their minds off all the junk food purposely displayed to entice them.

They should learn at a young age that the purpose of a shopping list is to save time and money. Most people who shop without a list tend to waste time wandering aimlessly throughout the store. They also tend to waste money because they are more likely to buy unnecessary items. They often toss unhealthy food and drinks into the cart, giving little thought to their actions.

The final temptations lay ahead as we approach the checkout lines. Impulse items such as chocolate, gum, candy bars, chips, and magazines are strategically placed near the registers. They are seemingly small inexpensive items that we just toss onto the moving conveyor. It may not seem like much, but a few dollars wasted here and there adds up over time.

Large corporations understand that those small inexpensive items can add up to billions of dollars in sales. Spending on small items can often do the most harm to our potential wealth because we place such little value on that money. How often have we said, "it's only $5 dollars?"

Another lesson to teach them is that a smart shopper is never caught off guard when the cashier taps the total button. One way to beat the register is to keep a running tally in your head as you shop. Round up that $8.49 package of meat to $9.00 and the $3.59 jar of peanut butter to $4.00. Then depending on the tax in your state, your bill should safely fall within your budgeted amount. If you prefer an exact count, you can put pen to paper or use a calculator to keep track of your spending.

Stop paying more than you planned. If you assumed the price of an item was lower, or you misread a sign, do not be ashamed to leave the item(s). You should never pay $20 dollars for an item you thought was $2 dollars because of pride.

***

A Message from Father Time

My dearest child – I was destined from birth to travel through life and to linger not, not even for you, my beloved. There is fairness in my heart, and I bestowed upon you the same twenty-four hours a day that I give to all my children. What you do with your gift is for you alone to decide.

On your journey through life you will meet many fascinating people. Be wary of the negative thoughts and actions of some. Be wary that their negative thoughts and actions do not become your own.

You will certainly run into ***Procrastination****. He is a laid-back, friendly sort of person, but do not be fooled by his mild manner. Procrastination will try to convince you to relax your mind and postpone your desires.*

It is his lot in life to drag his feet; the put-off-until-tomorrow thinking is his mindset. If you should choose to listen to him and accept his thoughts, the behavior of Procrastination will become your behavior—in which case, my adored one, I will surely leave you behind.

You will no doubt run into the ***Excuses Family****. They dwell within the soul of* ***A Lack of Responsibility****. The family does not realize that my purpose is to flee while they squander and ignore me, choosing instead to hang out with the likes of* ***Mr. and Mrs. Because****. The Excuses Family always has a reason, justification, or defense to explain their behavior.*

Wherever you find the Excuses, their good friend and neighbor, ***Mr. Cannot****, is never far behind. Mr. Cannot is not a bad person, per se, unlike you, he lacks ability. Mr. Cannot is filled with self-doubt and must accept his fate. So strong is his desire to hold you back that he will spend all his strength trying to convince you that you should not dream. You must not sacrifice me in order to debate with him; allow your actions to speak for you. Your achievements will become his weakness, and he will move on to another.*

You will also meet great men on your journey such as ***Sir Opportunity****. He, like me, will not linger. It has been said that he knocks but once. If you give him cause, however, he may return. Sir Opportunity is generous and wants you to succeed. He keeps company with wise men such as* ***Knowledge****,* ***Preparation****, and* ***Determination****. Information, Readiness, and Purpose, each man powerful in his own right — united they become a serious force.*

You must choose your friends wisely, dear one. You can rise or fall with those you call friends: But be wary, for some foes will come to you in the form of friends. ***Bad Habit*** *is a dangerous opponent that may come to you in the form of a charming companion. Bad Habit has a special quality that seems to delight and attract those around him. His true nature is revealed only after he has instilled negative behavior patterns in his victim - taking delight in the fact that he has fulfilled his mission. It is wise to put great distance between yourself and such a person. A Bad Habit is easier to avoid than to break.*

Failure *is unhappy and wants others to join him in his misery. Failure may stick out his foot and trip you as you run toward your goals. You get up and continue the race only to lose your footing and have Failure push you to the ground.*

Failure smiles when you fall. His goal is to knock you down again and again with the hope that you give up and stay down, thereby allowing him to fulfill his purpose. Getting knocked down is not failure. Whether or not to get up is a choice only you alone can make.

On your journey, ***Forgiveness*** *will be your ally against* ***Bitterness****. Welcome her friendship. Bitterness will try to capture and keep me a prisoner frozen in resentment and anger. By not holding on to negative emotions, you, and only you, have the power to ensure that I remain free to fulfill my destiny.*

Be mindful that ***A New Day*** *is on your side, always eager to give you the chance to brush yourself off and rise once more.* ***Yesterday*** *moved on and does not linger to rub your face in what was or what might have been.* ***Tomorrow*** *is selfish and promises himself to no one. The* ***Future*** *awaits, make of it what you will.*

Many of my children have said to me, "But Father, I need just a little more of you, I did not mean to forsake you. I did not mean to let you get away." My heart breaks for all those that I have left behind, but I must keep moving, I feel the gentle breeze of the wind pushing me forward.

I was destined to travel through life and to linger not —
not even for you, my beloved.

Father Time

Chapter Seven

Financial Jargon:
An Introduction to the Cast and Crew

I am...my thoughts.

Those of you with inquiring minds will dig deeper into the backgrounds of this amazing cast, learning more about what makes them powerful & fabulous. Do not be intimidated by all the fancy names and financial mumbo jumbo. They are all just different ways to save money.

First Lady Cash

Money, Money, Money

An Emergency Fund

An emergency fund is money that we set aside to be used in the event of an unexpected situation — such as a job loss, car repairs, dental work, etc. Any time extra money is needed.

An Asset

An Asset is anything of financial value such as Stocks and Bonds that you own and can exchange for *cash*.

Liability

A liability is a financial responsibility. It is anything that cost you money to own or use. Most of us need a reliable car to get around. Driving around in a costly dream car that takes years to pay for, however, can be very expensive.

Wealth

Wealth is having a large quantity of *money* and *assets and* owning items that have financial value.

Stocks and Bonds

When you buy stock or shares, you are buying a piece of a company. The more stock or shares you buy in a company, the more of that company you own. Owning a piece of a company or stock means that you have a claim on the company's assets and earnings. If the company makes money, then you make money.

When you buy bonds, you are lending money to a government, city or town, company, federal agency or other entity known as an issuer. For lending them money, the issuer gives you a bond/note promising to pay you a certain rate of interest during the life of the bond in addition to the principal amount of money that you lent them.

Certificates of Deposit (CDs)

CDs are just another way to save money. CDs usually pay a fixed interest rate. Interest rates are quite low right now. You can hold CDs until they mature and then you can withdraw the money, including the accrued interest, or you can reinvest the money.

Mutual Funds

A mutual fund is thousands of small investors putting our money together to buy stocks, bonds, or other securities. You will normally pay monthly fees with mutual funds.

Annuity

An Annuity is an investment vehicle sold by insurance companies. An Annuity pays the investor a set amount of money each year.

401(k)

A 401(k) is a defined retirement plan account. Through payroll deductions, you can invest a percentage of your earnings before or after taxes are deducted from your paycheck. With a 401(k), most employers will contribute money up to a certain amount or percentage: free money.

There are two types of IRAs (Individual Retirement Accounts):

Roth IRA

A Roth IRA is another way to save money for your retirement. You can open a Roth IRA if you have taxable earned income (a job) and qualify under the income limits. The great thing about a Roth IRA is that the money is tax-free when you start making withdrawals. An IRA is a great way to introduce your working teen to the world of personal finance.

Traditional IRA

A Traditional IRA is a personal savings plan for your retirement. With a Traditional IRA, the government gives us a tax benefit or tax break for setting money aside for our retirement. Because you get a tax break upfront, a Traditional IRA is taxed when you start making withdrawals.

Consumer Debt

The most common forms of consumer debt are credit card debt and loans. The problem is that a large portion of consumer debt is created because we borrow money to purchase items that have very little financial value such as clothes, furniture, dining out, etc. We have been conditioned to become payment buyers; just charge it and then make payments for years.

Loan

A loan is when you borrow money from a bank, financial establishment, family member or a friend.

Interest

Interest is a fee, the price that we pay for borrowing money. Paying interest on items that have no financial value will greatly slow down the wealth-building process. The more money you are repaying to someone else, the less money you will have to pay yourself.

Financial Freedom

Financial freedom is having enough money and assets so you do not need to depend on others for your living expenses.

Personal Finance

Personal finance is the way you manage your household money and the way you pay your bills, save, and invest, etc.

Budget

A budget is a detailed schedule of your spending. It is a tool to help you take charge of the money coming in and out of your household.

Expenses

Expenses, like liabilities, cost you money. Expenses are an outflow of money. Because they are normally items that we consume, they generally do not have a resale value. Examples of expenses are such items as cable service, cell phone payments, and food, etc.

Appreciate

When an item appreciates, it increases in value. For example, if you purchase a house for $150,000 and it is later worth $175,000, your house has appreciated or gone up in value.

Depreciate

Depreciate is the opposite of appreciate. When something depreciates, it decreases in value, meaning it is worth less than what you paid. Cars, clothes, furniture, boats, electronics, and toys are examples of items that will lose value by the time you get home. A house can also depreciate. If you purchase a house for $375,000 and it is later worth $350,000, your house has depreciated/gone down in value.

Contract

A contract is when you enter into a legal agreement either in writing or oral that is enforceable by law. Keep in mind that it must be a legal agreement. You cannot hire someone to steal a television and expect to have the agreement enforced if he or she fails to deliver.

Credit

Credit gives us the ability to buy the things that we really cannot afford. Credit is a loan that creates debt or the ability to receive goods or services before we pay. A furniture store may allow you to take home a bedroom set with the agreement that you will pay in the future.

Debt

Debt is created anytime you borrow money. If you want your money to grow, keeping your debt low is important.

Secured Debt

Secured debt means that the creditor (the person or company that lent you money) can take back their property if you default on the loan (fail to repay as promised). The most common secured debts are for homes and cars.

If you fail to keep up with your mortgage payments, the lender can foreclose on (take possession of) your home. If you fail to meet your financial obligations on your car, the lender has the right to take back the vehicle.

The joke is on us. The creditor really owns the property (until we make the final payment), but we get the responsibility of ownership: the maintenance, taxes, providing insurance, and everything else that goes along with true ownership.

Unsecured Debt

With unsecured debt, the creditor does not have the right to repossess the property if you fail to repay the loan. The creditor does have the right, however, to sue and try to get a judgment against you. Merchandise purchased with credit cards falls under the category of unsecured debt.

Principal

When you borrow money or take out a loan, the principal is the initial amount of money that you borrowed before interest and fees are added.

For example, if you borrow $500:
$500 is the principal or loan amount
$50 interest (random numbers used for representation only)

Total amount paid: $500 + $50 = $550

Interest

Interest is the cost of borrowing money or receiving credit.

Simple Interest

Simple interest is the amount of money you pay for your loan. Simple interest is common with auto loans; normally there is no penalty for repaying the loan early.

Fixed-Rate Interest Loan

With a fixed-rate loan, your interest and monthly payments remain the same during the life of the loan. Because your payments stay the same each month, it is easier to create a budget.

Adjustable-Rate Interest Loan

With an adjustable-rate interest loan, your payments will rise or fall depending on the interest rates in the economy.

Teaser-Rate Loan

With a teaser rate, the lender may discount the interest at the beginning of the loan to give you lower payments. A gimmick to get your business. Eventually, they will phase out the discount rate and your payments may increase.

A Balloon Payment

A balloon payment is a large lump sum that is normally due at the end of the loan. Balloon loans can commonly be found in mortgage loans, so always read the fine print. The balloon payment covers the loan amount that the payments do not cover. Balloon payments are often used to keep monthly payments low.

Default

A financial default is when you fail to repay your legally binding contract within a specified time.

Repossession

A repossession occurs when you fail to meet your financial obligation and the lender takes back their property. If you stop making your payments as agreed, you are in default and the lender has the right to seize their property. Cars are famous for being repossessed, so much so that there are television shows based on the repossession of vehicles.

Discretionary Income

Discretionary income is the money you have left over after you have paid your taxes, deductions, and living expenses.

Predatory Lending

Predatory lending is the practice of convincing potential borrowers to take out overpriced, high-interest loans when they qualify for standard loans. This is a reason that educating yourself is important before you sign any contracts.

***

The Illustrious Compound Interest

Albert Einstein said, "*The most powerful force in the universe is compound interest.*" Given enough time and patience even modest returns can generate wealth. The structure of compound interest is such that your money feeds on itself, first paying interest on your principal, then earning interest on the previous interest.

For example, if you invest $1,000 (principal investment) at 5 percent compound interest: $1,000 earning 5 percent interest = $50. The $50 is added to the original principal: $1,000 + $50 = $1,050.

- The next time you earn interest, you will earn interest on *both* the principal and the interest you previously earned. Your new principal amount is $1,050.

You now have $1,050 earning 5 percent interest = $52.50. The $52.50 is added to your new principal amount: $1,050 + $52.50 = $1,102.50.

- Your new principal is $1,102.50 earning 5 percent interest = $55.13. The $55.13 is added to your new principal amount: $1,102.50 + $55.13 = $1,157.63.

The dark side of compound interest comes when we are paying it instead of earning it. Compound interest is the main reason we spend so many years trapped on a negative financial treadmill. Credit card debt is an example of the dark side of compound interest.

***

A Personal Balance Sheet

A Personal Balance Sheet consists of three parts:
Assets - Liabilities = Equity (A - L = E)

Your Assets (what you own), minus **Your Liabilities** (what you owe) = **Equity** (the remaining value of your assets once you pay your financial obligations).

A Personal Balance Sheet is a list of your current **Assets** or things that you **own** that have financial value. In other words, something that can be exchanged for the lovely cash! Your list of assets can include items such as the money in your checking account, savings, stocks, bonds, and real estate, etc.

Your Personal Balance Sheet also includes what you owe; These are your financial obligations that are also known as **Liabilities**. **Equity** is what is left after you pay your financial obligations.

Taking the first step on the road to financial independence will be the most difficult step on the journey. It is easy to sit back, complain, and do nothing to improve your life. Creating fabulous credit takes a *Diva State of Mind.*

There are millions of women who want their financial life to improve; unfortunately, they do not want it bad enough to do the work. If you really want to become a Financially Fabulous Diva, then you must want it bad enough to do the work.

***

What is a Credit Score?

A credit score, also known as a FICO (Fair Isaac Corporation) score, is a three-digit number that is calculated based on your credit/payment history. **It ranges from 250 to 900**. (Note: There is also another score called a Vantage Score. A Vantage Score can range from 501 to 990 but may not reflect your true score.)

The purpose of your Credit Score is to help lenders determine if they should extend credit or lend money to you. To put it simply, the lender wants to have an idea of just how likely you are to repay their money. Your score will also determine how much you pay for a loan (interest rate). A low score may mean that you are too much of a risk, and your loan request could be denied.

Five factors determine your credit score; the two most important factors are your payment/credit history and how much you currently owe.

1.) Thirty-five percent (35 percent) of your credit score is based on your payment history. Your **payment history** shows a creditor if you have a habit of paying your bills late or on time. It tells a creditor if you have bills that you have **not** paid and have been sent to collection agencies. It also shows creditors if you've had a car or other item repossessed because you failed to pay. A bankruptcy in your history will greatly hurt your score.

2.) Thirty percent (30 percent) of your credit score is based on your outstanding debt: your **outstanding debt** is how much you owe on your credit cards, an auto loan, or your home loan/mortgage.

3.) Fifteen percent (15 percent) of your credit score is based on **how long you've had credit**. (How many years you've had your credit card—or how long you've been making payments on an auto loan).

4.) Ten percent (10 percent) of your credit score is based on the **number of inquiries.** Each time you fill out an application to borrow money (loan) or apply for a credit card, you are giving a bank or financial institution permission to check your credit report. The credit bureaus keep a record of those inquiries.

5.) Ten percent (10 percent) of your credit score is based on the types of credit that you have, such as: student loans, credit cards, auto or home loans/mortgage, etc.

Fabulous Credit:
Your Financial Report Card

What is a Credit Report?

A credit report is an intimate look at the way you handle your money. Think of it as a financial report card from the lenders that you borrowed money from, and/or have extended credit to you. This report includes your account balances (past and present) and shows if you make payments on time.

Your credit report will also show if any action was taken against you for unpaid bills. It will show if you did not pay a debt and your account was sent to a collection agency, or if a creditor foreclosed property or repossessed a car for nonpayment.

What is in your Credit Report?

The format may be different, but credit reporting agencies supply the same categories of information:

Identifying Information

Your name and any aliases
Your current and previous addresses
Your social security number and date of birth
Your employment information

These items on your credit report are updated with information that you supply to lenders. This information does not affect your credit score.

Trade Lines/Credit Accounts
Each time you open and establish an account with a lender, the lending institution reports several things to credit reporting agencies:

- The type of accounts you opened: i.e. credit card, auto loan, student loan, mortgage, etc.,
- The date you opened or closed the account;
- The amount of the loan and/or the amount of your credit limit;

- The account balance and your payment history.

The report also includes a list of late payments that were 30, 60, 90, or 120-plus days late.

Credit Inquiries

Each time you apply for a loan or credit card, you authorize a lender to ask for a copy of your credit report. The inquiries section contains a list of those lenders. Giving a lender permission to view your credit report should only be done when you are ready and able to do business with that institution. Your credit report contains important and valuable information and should not be given out lightly.

The next time someone offers you a 10 or 20 percent discount if you apply for their credit card – just say thanks, but no thanks! The interest rate on that store credit card could be as high as 36 percent!

Public Record Information

Public records are also shown in your credit report. State and county records, information on tax liens, bankruptcies, or monetary judgments are included.

Free Credit Report

Once a year, by US law, you are entitled to request a FREE copy of your credit report. Beware! Many companies charge a fee for this information when it is available to you for FREE.

Your credit report does not include your **Credit Score**. Your score is available for a reasonable fee when you get your credit report.

There are three main credit reporting bureaus:

TransUnion

Experian

Equifax

To receive your free copies, contact each of the three main credit bureaus by phone, mail, or go to the official website at

www.annualcreditreport.com

Insurance: Protecting Our Loved Ones

Not many people want to talk about death or the need for life insurance. Most people tend to shy away from such morbid topics. Death, however, is the only way to depart life's stage. We can take our final bow comforted by the knowledge that we have left our family financially secure.

Or, we can leave our loved ones penniless and at the mercy of friends and relatives.

What is the purpose of life insurance? The main purpose of life insurance is to protect the people who depend on us financially and to help pay off our financial obligations. We may not realize how important life insurance is until there is an unexpected death in the family; suddenly, we are reminded that a long and healthy life is not promised.

Ask yourself if you need life insurance. Does anyone depend on you financially? How much insurance coverage do you need? How much insurance can you afford? Are you married with children?

If so, what would happen to your family if they lost not only you, but also the income that you provide? How would your family survive without your earnings? Would they be able to pay the mortgage or rent without your revenue?

Who takes care of the children? Do you need life insurance coverage on the parent who stays home to raise the children? Would you need to hire someone to do the work that the stay-at-home parent or caregiver is providing for the family?

You may not appreciate the value that a person brings to the home until he or she is no longer in your life. Are you a stay-at-home parent dependent on someone else financially? How would you survive in the event of their death? Could you afford to remain in your home if the breadwinner died unexpectedly? Would your children's education suffer?

Life insurance can also provide monetary assistance to bury a family member. Trying to raise money for funeral expenses after the fact is added stress to an already difficult time.

Consider the high cost of a memorial service. The owners of the funeral home are not being insensitive in your time of need when they question your ability to pay. It is nothing personal, it is their “business”.

If you are a parent with or without the benefit of marriage, it may be wise to have life insurance on the co-parent, as well as yourself. The child or children will still need to be provided for in the event of a death. Needless to say, you cannot receive child support from the great beyond. The best time to discuss life insurance, if you are not married, is when love is in the air. He or she may not be inclined to discuss life insurance with you if you are no longer in a relationship.

The well-being and financial security of the children should be your main concern. Take the time to find the policy that is best for your family. Taking the time to research life insurance and figuring out which type is best for you and your family is well worth the time and energy that you invest.

Also, keep in mind that while it is great to have a life insurance policy with your employer, many policies will end with the job. It may be better to have a life insurance policy that is not contingent upon you working for a particular company.

Do not leave your loved ones holding the bag because of poor choices. If you do not have anyone who depends on you financially, you will at least need enough coverage to handle your burial and financial obligations.

If you have a family member or child who is not responsible, you need to make sure they have life insurance even if you must pay the premiums yourself. Paying a few dollars a month is less expensive than coming up with thousands of dollars later to pay for their funeral.

Discussing insurance with loved ones will not put you on the fast track to death. Talking about, and preparing for, the inevitable, is the responsible thing to do.

***

Temporary Life Insurance

Temporary life insurance, best known as **term life** insurance, is just what the name implies: temporary or for a limited time. You may have children and want life insurance to keep them protected until they become of age or are out of college.

Term insurance, also referred to as **pure insurance**, can be purchased in increments from one to thirty years (a block of time that best serves your family). Term life insurance costs less than whole life. If you have a five-year-old, you may want term insurance for twenty years or until he or she completes college.

Premiums (payments) can be made monthly, quarterly, semiannually, or annually. Term insurance will pay your beneficiary the face value of the policy when you die.

***

Whole Life Insurance

Whole life insurance covers you for the duration of your life, as long as you keep up your premiums and your policy has not been cancelled. Whole life insurance is more expensive because it includes an investment feature that builds cash value.

You can borrow against the cash value. But that is equivalent to borrowing your own money and paying someone else interest. It also takes years to build up a decent cash value.

Long before I knew anything about life insurance, I purchased a whole life insurance policy to cover my children in the event something happened to them. After learning a little more about life insurance, I cancelled the policy and replaced it with term insurance. The cash buildup after four years was only $9.50, hardly worth the higher premiums of the whole life policy.

***

Renters Insurance

One day my youngest daughter's apartment flooded and I ended up having an unexpected houseguest. It turns out the apartment on the other side of her shared wall had a pipe burst and flooded not only her apartment, but also two others.

When we arrived at her apartment, the manager of the complex was already there with all the other displaced renters and the emergency cleanup crew. The very first things out of the mouth of the apartment manager were: "You do know that we are not liable for your belongings," and "Do you have **renter's insurance**?"

When my daughter responded that she did indeed have renter's insurance, the manager let out a deep sigh of relief. "Oh, thank goodness, I love this girl!" she said, looking at me.

Fortunately, she was able to save most of her belongings. The cost to pack and deliver her items to her new apartment was a few thousand dollars, and thankfully was covered by her insurance. The policy also covered the cost of a hotel room and food while she looked for a new place to live.

Having renter's insurance made a stressful situation bearable. Knowing I did not have to deal with that situation made me very happy. You will not profit from having insurance, of course, but the financial assistance is wonderful.

You do not want to depend on a government agency or the kindness of neighbors for assistance when affordable insurance can save the day in the event of a flood, fire, or other unforeseen damage to your rented housing.

Do not assume that the property owner's insurance will cover your belongings or provide you with housing in an emergency. In my daughter's case, the pipes that burst were the property of the apartment owners.

Flood or no flood, they would have expected her to pay rent as long as her wet belongings were in their apartment. Because she had insurance, she was able to go to work, leaving the professionals to deal with the cleanup.

So, run your household like a business. Get the insurance that you need to protect yourself and your family. Renters insurance is very affordable.

Discount Dental Plans

What is a Discount Dental Plan? It is just what the name states — a dental discount plan. A Dental Discount Plan is NOT dental insurance. Think of it as having a coupon. The plans offer individual as well as family coverage. It is a great way to help you save money at the dentist.

It is difficult to overstate the advantages of a Dental Discount Plan. You can be sitting in the waiting room with ten other people and because of a little information and research about dental plans, pay hundreds, or even thousands, of dollars less for the same procedure performed by the same dentist.

I saw dental discount plans advertised for years, but never took the time to get additional information. To be honest, I did not think the plan was legit but I was very wrong.

Because it is not dental insurance, you do not have to worry about filling out complex paperwork or wait to be reimbursed. The plans cover preventive treatments such as cleanings and sealants.

The plans also work on major procedures such as root canals and bridges. Do you need extractions or dentures? Good news! Many plans offer a discount for dentures (uppers and lowers). You can restore your smile and save money.

Did I mention that the Dental Discount Plans are very affordable? If not, then here it is: the plans are very affordable. Do not waste time thinking about it or putting it off. Information is power and a money saver.

Do yourself and your family a favor by researching the benefits of becoming a member of a Dental Plan. Many of the plans also include vision and prescriptions for an additional fee.

With most of the plans, you can print your ID and head to the dentist within a week. You can actually speak with a live person to get answers to your questions.

***

You've reached...
A Financial Turning Point.

There is Power...

in Setting Financial Goals.

Made in the USA
Monee, IL
04 November 2026

67377399R00095